The Snark Handbook

INSULT EDITION

Also by Lawrence Dorfman

The Snark Handbook
The Cigar Lover's Compendium

The Snark Handbook

INSULT EDITION

COMEBACKS, TAUNTS, AND EFFRONTERIES

LAWRENCE DORFMAN

Skyhorse Publishing

Skyhorse Publishing books may be purchased in bulk at special discounts for sales promotion, corporate gifts, fund-raising, or educational purposes. Special editions can also be created to specifications. For details, contact the Special Sales Department, Skyhorse Publishing, 555 Eighth Avenue, Suite 903, New York, NY 10018 or info@skyhorsepublishing.com.

www.skyhorsepublishing.com

10 9 8 7 6 5 4 3

Library of Congress Cataloging-in-Publication Data

Dorfman, Lawrence.
  The snark handbook : insult edition : comebacks, taunts, and effronteries / Lawrence Dorfman.
      p. cm.
  Includes bibliographical references and index.
  ISBN 978-1-61608-059-4 (pbk. : alk. paper)
  1. Invective--Humor. I. Title.
  PN6231.I65D674 2009
  808.87--dc22

                              2010025004
Printed in China

This book is both good and original.
But the part that is good is not original and the
part that is original is not good.
—SAMUEL JOHNSON

When you're born, you get a ticket to the freak show. When
you're born in America, you get a front-row seat.
—HUNTER S. THOMPSON

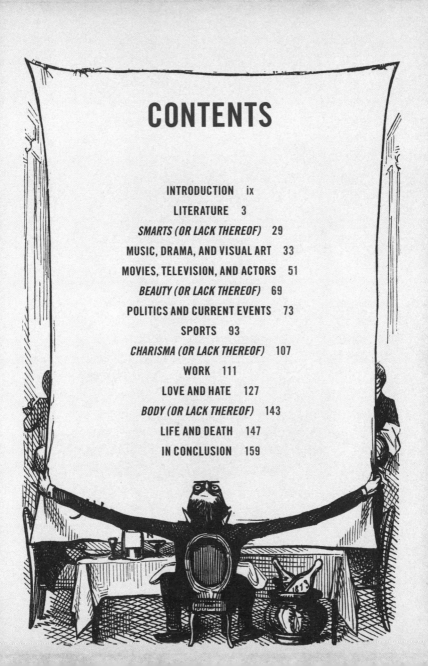

CONTENTS

He's just another flash in the bedpan. • She couldn't exude warmth if she was

Introduction

WELL, HERE WE GO AGAIN . . . and just when you thought it was safe to go back in the water.

When my publisher called and said *The Snark Handbook* was selling and that we needed to start thinking about the next book in the "series," my first thought was, "Since when was this a series?" and then, "Enough already, ya greedy bastids" . . . but they persisted. And so, dear reader, you have before you *The Snark Handbook: Insult Edition*.

"Hey, Lar," one might ask . . . "weren't there a lot of insults in the first book?"[1]

Yes, there were a few. Placed strategically at the bottom of each page was a CNN-like running ticker tape of snarky insults, geared toward the mid-level intellect for quick and easy use. What about it?

---

[1]   Who are you, Sherlock Holmes?

. ✦ You'll have to excuse him. He's going through a nonentity crisis. ✦ The terrifying

What I intend to tell you with this second, clearly exploitative book is that the insult can be, and is, so much, much more.

It can be your friend, your protector, your sword, your shield . . . all that and a bag of chips.

Whence It Came

So, when did Man start insulting each other? Probably that day that Gork brought back a brontosaurus steak that was just a little too skimpy for the rest of the tribe's taste . . . "Hey, we gonna eat that or make it into a wallet?" . . . then again, probably not.

I think it was Freud who said, "The first human who hurled an insult instead of a stone was the founder of civilization" . . . whatever.

Going back many years, one can find the insult starting to find its niche as early as the mid-1500s, with words like "ninny," "dunderhead," "simpleton," "numbskull," "nincompoop," and "blockhead" showing up in literature and in the records of daily use. Used liberally by Shakespeare on down, the insult was primarily a phrase used to speak to one's lack of intellect or knowledge . . .

Hey, who knew the Three Stooges were literary scholars?

Over the years, the insult began to evolve. Used to great effect in vaudeville and in the first talkies, the insult started to take hold as a way of putting your enemies off their game and bringing the audience into the joke, usually against the hapless recipient of the stinging barb. Cream pies in the face, while certainly insulting, just weren't enough. People wanted words. And words they got.

I'm going to go out on a limb here and call Groucho Marx the first reigning king of the sarcastic insult. For those of you who are growing up on Jon Stewart, Groucho was Stewart times ten. He had a scathing wit, rapid-fire delivery, and a liberal way with innuendo.

Bringing It Home

We start young: hanging out and constantly making fun of our friends—their clothes, looks, music, girlfriends, other friends. Call it "dissing" or "playing the dozens." Whatever you call it, it doesn't make it any less nasty. You're out to draw blood, symbolically, to prove your superiority. What makes it snarky is that element of the in-joke. If your friends didn't get it—like the people who aren't your friends who might well be listening—it wouldn't be quite so fun.

As we got older and began to censor ourselves (or be censored by the surrounding conventions—work, home,

ling to father you. • A sharp tongue is no indication of a keen mind. • Everyone is

The Snark Handbook: Insult Edition

school), we began to use sarcasm and innuendo. . . . always a treat but perhaps a bit more subtle than what you're going to find here.[2]

The snarky insult, however, lets you get it all off your chest. It gives you the upper hand . . . and lets you keep it. It keeps the wolf from the door. It avoids beating around the bush. It cuts to the chase.[3] It says, "You're not getting away with that". . . or "are you really going to do/say that?" or "don't you realize what a schmuck you are?"

How to Do It

So where do we start? Maybe with a few basic rules . . .

1. Everything takes a backseat to wit and cleverness. You want to make people think . . . and then think twice.
2. Start by listening. Pay close attention to people. Besides alerting you to when you're being insulted, it's also a good way to find the fodder for the barbs you want to throw back.
3. Respond immediately. The moment comes and the moment passes. Jump in. In this book are tons of insults. Memorize as many as you can and use them to full effect.

---

[2] See example A, *The Snark Handbook*, for subtle snark.
[3] It can even cut the chase.

gifted. Some open the package sooner. ◆ It may be that your whole purpose in life

The Insult Hall of Shame

As mentioned above, there were many players over the years but a select few achieved the kind of status that is only awarded to the most vitriolic of the bunch. In the late nineteenth century, with the advent of vaudeville, and years later, Vegas, the insult became a great source of comedy. The best and the brightest:[4]

Oscar Wilde (1854–1900): A serpent-tongued Irish writer who eventually became heralded as one of the greatest playwrights the world has known. Ridiculed in his day, he died broke at age forty-six.

————

Winston Churchill (1874–1965): The great statesman of the putdown. A speech impediment at a young age made him crotchety.

————

Groucho Marx[5] (1890–1970): Rapid-fire insults before TiVo, so you needed to listen carefully. The undisputed master of the snark.

———————

[4] By no means complete, like a hundred politicians at the bottom of the ocean, it's a good start.

[5] Groucho's father, Simon, worked as a tailor, but since he refused to use a measuring tape, his customers were seldom satisfied. True story.

ply to serve as a warning to others. • You fill a much-needed gap. • You have the

Mae West (1893–1980): Queen of the throwaway barb. A buxom, zaftig movie star with an inferred sex life that was turned up to eleven.

———

Dorothy Parker (1893–1967): A lifelong member of the Algonquin Round Table, Ms. Parker had an acerbic speed-of-light wit that was often turned on anyone around her.

———

The Three Stooges: Moe (1897–1975), Larry (1902–1975), and Curly (1903–1952): (I don't count Curly Joe or Joe Besser—Shemp is on the bubble). Mostly physical insults but lots of name-calling, too. Pick two fingers.

———

Don Rickles (1926–present): The undisputed master of the insult.[6] Unlike many insult comics, who only find short-lived success, Rickles has enjoyed a sustained career in insult performance. Rickles was king of the quick comeback and the vitriolic putdown.

———

The Friars Roast (1950–present): Legitimizing the caustic putdown, all in "good fun." Most recently a staple of Comedy Central, where the gloves have clearly been taken off and

---

[6]   Yeah, there's two masters . . . what about it?

———

Midas touch. Everything you touch turns to muffler. • If he were any more stupid, h

anything goes. Breeding ground for the great, the near-great, and the grating.

———

Dennis Miller (1953–present): Cerebral comic whose subtle references could make your head spin.

———

Denis Leary (1957–present): Started out as a Boston comic then turned a bigger public on to ranting on MTV and then took off.

———

Andrew Dice Clay (1957–present): The insult comic as rock star . . . appealed to the lowest common denominator, but, man, he could be funny.

———

Bill Hicks (1961–1994): His jokes included general discussions about society, religion, politics, philosophy, and personal issues. Hicks's material was often deliberately controversial and quite insulting.

———

Lisa Lampanelli (1961–present): The latest in a long line of insult comics. Sold-out concerts make her the new Dice Clay.

———

Jeffrey Ross (1965–present): The Friars Club's honorary "Roastmaster" and clearly a student of the "old school" of insult comedy.

to be watered twice a week. • I'd like to give you a going-away present . . . but you

———

Triumph the Insult Comic Dog (1997–present): The brain-child of Robert Smigel of *Saturday Night Live* fame, this puppet dog started on Late Night with Conan O'Brien and soon took off with his own DVDs and appearances.

———

This is the bar, set high. Go ahead, Snarky. See if you can clear it.

have to do your part. ◆ I can tell you are lying. Your lips are moving. ◆ I don't r

AUTHOR'S NOTE

S O, EVIDENTLY, I'VE BECOME a minor celebrity since the first book pubbed. And I *am* talkin' minor . . . that kid that got rescued out of the well a few years back gets more attention these days than I do. . . . I know, deal with it, ya whiny snark baby.

Anyway . . . I started a daily snark on Facebook (*The Snark Handbook*) where I make snarky comments about what's happening in the news that makes me cranky.

I've included a few in the book, the timeless ones that will make sense, long after the celebrities that pass for news stories these days are in the retired B-list entertainers' home. Called *Snarkin' the News*, you too can play along, either on FB or by starting your own. It's fun, it's enlightening (gotta read the papers, Bernstein), and it's just pennies a day (not really, it's free) . . .

Enjoy. Or don't.

saying, but I just don't care. ◆ If what you don't know can't hurt you, she's practi

The Snark Handbook

INSULT EDITION

the last mosquito that bit him had to check into the Betty Ford Clinic. ✦ In

Literature

Fine words! I wonder where you stole them.
—JONATHAN SWIFT

THE LITERATI TEND TO be more cultured . . . but not a whole lot more. More often than not, they say in a multitude of sentences what should be said to better effect in one or two. Most expel more wind than a hot-air balloon.

The quotes here are where the so-called "best and brightest" hold forth and let the vitriol fly. Clearly, book learning doesn't mean a better class of people. Some of these are downright evil. Can't wait, huh? Good stuff . . . and all very usable in day-to-day verbal combat.

Nature, not content with denying him the
ability to think, has endowed him with the
ability to write.
—A. E. HOUSMAN

+++

Ordinarily he is insane. But he has lucid moments
when he is only stupid.
—HEINRICH HEINE

++

She and her sex had better mind the kitchen and her
children; and perhaps the poor; except in such things as
little novels, they only devote themselves to what men do
much better, leaving that which men do worse or not at all.
—EDWARD FITZGERALD ON ELIZABETH
BARRETT BROWNING

+++

If a person is not talented enough to be a novelist, not
smart enough to be a lawyer, and his hands are too shaky to
perform operations, he becomes a journalist.
—NORMAN MAILER

++

Everywhere I go I'm asked if I think the university stifles
writers. My opinion is that they don't stifle enough of them.
—FLANNERY O'CONNOR

Any reviewer who expresses rage and loathing for a novel is preposterous. He or she is like a person who has put on full armor and attacked a hot fudge sundae.[7]
—KURT VONNEGUT

~+~

Edna Ferber, one of the brightest lights in the New York "Algonquin Round Table Group" of the twenties and thirties, had a penchant for wearing elegantly tailored suits, trousers and all. Noël Coward met her one day in New York when he was wearing a suit very similar to the one Miss Ferber was sporting. "Edna, you look almost like a man," he told her. "So do you," she answered.

~+~

He is the same old sausage, fizzing and sputtering in his own grease.
—HENRY JAMES

+++

You're a mouse studying to be a rat.
—WILSON MIZNER

---

[7]   Hey Kurt, relax. If Attila the Hun were alive today he'd be a critic.

does the scum.   •   The thing that terrifies me the most is that someone might hate me

Match the Criticism to the Book[8]

A. *Paradise Lost*   D. *Uncle Tom's Cabin*
   (John Milton)   (Harriet Beecher Stowe)
B. *Three Lives*   E. *Franny and Zooey*
   (Gertrude Stein)   (J. D. Salinger)
C. *Moby-Dick*   F. *A Man in Full*
   (Herman Melville)   (Tom Wolfe)

~•~

1. Nobody can be more clownish, more clumsy and sententiously in bad taste . . . Oh dear, when the solemn ass brays! brays! brays! —D. H. Lawrence

2. A cold suet-roll of fabulously reptilian length. Cut it at any point, it is the same thing; the same heavy, sticky, opaque mass all through and all along. —Wyndham Lewis

3. The book has gas and runs out of gas, fills up again, goes dry. It is a 742-page work that reads as if it is fifteen hundred pages long. . . . —Norman Mailer

4. One of the books which the reader admires and lays down, and forgets to take up again. None ever wished it longer than it is. —Samuel Johnson

5. So you're the little woman who wrote the book that made this great war. —Abraham Lincoln

---

8   1. C., 2. B., 3. F., 4. A., 5. D., 6. E.

as much as I loathe you. • He has the most remarkable and seductive genius—a

6. It suffers from this terrible sort of metropolitan senti-
   mentality and it's so narcissistic . . . so false, so calculated.
   Combining the plain man with an absolutely megaloma-
   niac egotism. I simply can't stand it. —Mary McCarthy

Mr. Huxley is perhaps one of
those people who have to perpetrate thirty bad novels before
producing a good one.
—T. S. ELIOT ON ALDOUS HUXLEY

♦♦

He knows so little and knows it so fluently.
—ELLEN GLASGOW

♦♦♦

He looked as inconspicuous as a tarantula on a
slice of angel food.
—RAYMOND CHANDLER

♦♦

We do not have to visit a madhouse to
find disordered minds; our planet is the mental institution
of the universe.
—JOHANN WOLFGANG VON GOETHE

ld say about the smallest in the world. ♦ If I were him I'd be less concerned with

A flabby lemon and pink giant, who hung his mouth open
as though he were an animal at the zoo inviting buns—
especially when the ladies were present.
—WYNDHAM LEWIS ON FORD MADOX FORD

❖❖❖

A book by Henry James is like a church lit but without
a congregation to distract you, with every light and line
focused on the high altar. And on the altar, very reverently
placed, intensely there, is a dead kitten, an eggshell,
a bit of string.
—H. G. WELLS

❖❖

Dorothy Parker

↔ That woman speaks eighteen languages and can't
say no in any of them.

↔ She looks like something that would eat its young.
(ON DAME EDITH EVANS)

↔ The affair between Margot Asquith and Margot
Asquith will live as one of the prettiest love stories
in all literature.

A louse in the locks of literature.
—LORD ALFRED TENNYSON
ON CRITIC CHURTON COLLINS

✦✦✦

He is a bad novelist and a fool. The combination usually
makes for great popularity in the U.S.
—GORE VIDAL ON ALEXANDER SOLZHENITSYN

✦✦

He missed an invaluable opportunity to hold his tongue.
—ANDREW LANG

✦✦✦

He was born stupid, and greatly increased his birthright.
—SAMUEL BUTLER

✦✦

He was one of those men who possess almost every gift,
except the gift of the power to use them.
—CHARLES KINGSLEY

✦✦✦

While he was not dumber than an ox he
was not any smarter either.
—JAMES THURBER

✦✦

He is not only dull himself, he is the cause of
dullness in others.
—SAMUEL JOHNSON

turned up any more, she'd blow off her hat every time she sneezed. ✦ If she holds her

Insults and More Insults

↔ He walked as if he had fouled his small clothes and looks as if he smelt it.[9]

↔ Mr. Eliot is at times an excellent poet and has arrived at the supreme Eminence among English critics largely through disguising himself as a corpse.[10]

↔ He was humane but not human.[11]

↔ He had a mind so fine that no idea could violate it.[12]

↔ I don't think Robert Browning was very good in bed. His wife probably didn't care for him very much. He snored and had fantasies about twelve-year-old girls.[13]

↔ Gibbon's style is detestable; but it is not the worst thing about him.[14]

[9] Christopher Smart on Thomas Gray
[10] Ezra Pound on T. S. Eliot
[11] e.e. cummings on Ezra Pound
[12] T. S. Eliot on Henry James
[13] W. H. Auden on Robert Browning
[14] Samuel Taylor Coleridge on Edward Gibbon

↔ An unmanly sort of man whose love-life seems to have been largely confined to crying in laps and playing mouse.[15]

↔ In conversation he is even duller than in writing, if that is possible.[16]

He is one of those people who would be enormously improved by death.
—H. H. MUNRO

♦♦

Nature played a cruel trick on her by giving her a waxed mustache.
—ALAN BENNETT

♦♦♦

Some folks are wise and some are otherwise.
—TOBIAS GEORGE SMOLLETT

♦♦

Some folks seem to have descended from the chimpanzee later than others.
—KIN HUBBARD

---

[15] W. H. Auden on Edgar Allan Poe
[16] Juliana Smith on Noah Webster

That's not writing; that's typing.[17]
—TRUMAN CAPOTE ON JACK KEROUAC

~•~

Clark Gable to William Faulkner: "Oh, Mr. Faulkner, do you write?" William Faulkner to Clark Gable: "Yes, I do, Mr. Gable. What do you do?"

~•~

His mind is so open that the wind whistles through it.
—HEYWOOD BROUN

•••

He must have had a magnificent build before his stomach went in for a career of its own.
—MARGARET HALSEY

••

I've just learned about his illness.
Let's hope it's nothing trivial.
—IRVIN S. COBB

•••

---

[17] This is ridiculous. Everyone knows you can't type on toilet paper.

to a point—the point of departure. • She'll talk her head off about confidences

He not only overflowed with learning,
but stood in the slop.
—SYDNEY SMITH

++

He was a solemn, unsmiling, sanctimonious
old iceberg who looked like he was waiting
for a vacancy in the Trilogy.
—MARK TWAIN

+++

His style has the desperate jauntiness of an orchestra
fiddling away for dear life on a sinking ship.
—EDMUND WILSON ON EVELYN WAUGH

++

His features resembled a fossilized washrag.
—ALAN BRIEN

+++

His ignorance covers the world like a blanket, and there's
scarcely a hole in it anywhere.
—MARK TWAIN

++

She's the triumph of sugar over diabetes.
—GEORGE JEAN NATHAN

Snarkin' the News

↬ HarperCollins is paying Scott Brown a lot of money to bare all in his memoirs. What happened to the days when you actually had to do something first to get a book deal? He'll have to wait and read his own book to find out what it is he's actually done.

↬ Other news: A judge ordered a Web site to remove a fictional story about a berserk giraffe that attacked a guide at a local zoo . . . perhaps because it was too hard to swallow?

↬ A copy of a *Superman #1* comic book sold recently for $1 million and nerds all over America could be heard yelling at their mothers for throwing their copies away when they cleaned out the basement.

His face was filled with broken commandments.
—JOHN MASEFIELD

✦✦✦

She's the sort of woman who lives for others—you can tell
the others by their hunted expression.
—C. S. LEWIS

horse—I'll be the head and you be yourself. ✦ The only thing that deprives her of th

Insults and More Insults

↔ He was a great friend of mine. Well, as much as you could be a friend of his, unless you were a fourteen-year-old nymphet.[18]

↔ A little emasculated mass of inanity.[19]

↔ He's a full-fledged housewife from Kansas with all the prejudices.[20]

↔ I am reading Henry James . . . and feel myself as one entombed in a block of smooth amber.[21]

↔ In her last days, she resembled a spoiled pear.[22]

↔ He is always willing to lend a helping hand to the ones above him. [23]

↔ I am fairly unrepentant about her poetry. I really think that three quarters of it is gibberish. However, I must crush down these thoughts; otherwise the dove of peace will shit on me.[24]

---

[18] Truman Capote on William Faulkner
[19] Theodore Roosevelt on Henry James
[20] Gore Vidal on Truman Capote
[21] Virginia Woolf on Henry James
[22] Gore Vidal on Gertrude Stein
[23] F. Scott Fitzgerald about Ernest Hemingway
[24] Noël Coward on Edith Sitwell

Match the Insult to the Book[25]

A. *The Idiot*
(Fyodor Dostoevsky)

B. *Pride and Prejudice*
(Jane Austen)

C. *Skinny Bitch*
(Freedman and
Barnouin)

D. *Lullaby*
(Chuck Palahniuk)

E. *Harry Potter and the
Prisoner of Azkaban*
(J. K. Rowling)

F. *Fear and Loathing in
Las Vegas*
(Hunter Thompson)

~✦~

1. You foul, loathsome, evil little cockroach.
2. You have delighted us long enough.
3. Maybe humans are just the pet alligators that God flushed down the toilet.
4. I hate you . . . you are the type, the incarnation, the acme of the most insolent and self-satisfied, the most vulgar and loathsome commonplaceness. Yours is the commonplaceness of pomposity, of self-satisfaction and olympian serenity. You are the most ordinary of the ordinary!
5. Is that a beard, or are you eating a muskrat?
6. Coffee is for pussies.

---

[25] 1. E., 2. B., 3. D., 4. A., 5. F., 6. C.

I worship the quicksand he walks in.
—ART BUCHWALD

~∗~

When Dorothy Parker was told that Calvin Coolidge had died, she asked: "How can they tell?"

~∗~

She could carry off anything; and
some people said that she did.
—ADA LEVERSON

∗∗

They hardly make 'em like him any more—but just to be on
the safe side, he should be castrated anyway.
—HUNTER S. THOMPSON

∗∗∗

He's as useless as a pulled tooth.
—MARY ROBERTS RINEHART

∗∗

He never chooses an opinion; he
just wears whatever happens to be in style.
—LEO TOLSTOY

He was a bit like a corkscrew.
Twisted, cold, and sharp.
—KATE CRUISE O'BRIEN

✦✦✦

He's a wit with dunces, and a dunce with wits.
—ALEXANDER POPE

✦✦

Oscar Wilde

↔ There are two ways of disliking poetry; one way is to dislike it, the other is to read Pope.

↔ He has no enemies, but is intensely disliked by his friends.

↔ Some cause happiness wherever they go; others whenever they go.

↔ Fashion is what one wears oneself. What is unfashionable is what other people wear.

↔ When the gods wish to punish us they answer our prayers.

↔ I don't recognize you—I've changed a lot.

↔ Only dull people are brilliant at breakfast.

you're ever invited is outside. ✦ He got a brain transplant, and the brain rejected him

↦ One should always be in love. This is the reason one should never marry.

↦ Fashion is a form of ugliness so intolerable that we have to alter it every six months.

↦ She is a peacock in everything but beauty.

↦ He hadn't a single redeeming vice.

↦ He has one of those characteristic British faces that, once seen, are never remembered.

↦ The play was a great success, but the audience was a disaster.

He has a brain of feathers, and a heart of lead.
—ALEXANDER POPE

✦✦✦

He had delusions of adequacy.
—WALTER KERR

✦✦

He was one of the nicest old ladies I ever met.
—WILLIAM FAULKNER

you are nobody's fool, but maybe someone will adopt you. ✦ I thought of you all day

The ineffable dunce has nothing to say and says it with a liberal embellishment of bad delivery, embroidering it with reasonless vulgarities of attitude, gesture, and attire. There never was an impostor so hateful, a blockhead so stupid, a crank so variously and offensively daft. He makes me tired.
—AMBROSE BIERCE ON OSCAR WILDE

✦✦✦

I want to reach your mind—where is it currently located?
—ASHLEIGH BRILLIANT

✦✦

Why don't you get a haircut?
You look like a chrysanthemum.
—P. G. WODEHOUSE

✦✦✦

She was a large woman who seemed
not so much dressed as upholstered.[26]
—JAMES MATTHEW BARRIE

✦✦

She was what we used to call a
suicide blonde—dyed by her own hand.
—SAUL BELLOW

---

[26] This from the guy who wrote *Peter Pan*?

today. I was at the zoo. ✦ I never forgot the first time we met—I keep t

Full Circle (ish) Snark

↔ **Sir Walter Scott, according to Mark Twain**
He did measureless harm; more real and lasting harm, perhaps, than any other individual that ever wrote.

↔ **Mark Twain, according to William Faulkner**
A hack writer who would not have been considered fourth rate in Europe, who tricked out a few of the old proven "sure-fire" literary skeletons with sufficient local color to intrigue the superficial and the lazy.

↔ **William Faulkner, according to Ernest Hemingway**
Have you ever heard of anyone who drank while he worked? You're thinking of Faulkner. He does sometimes—and I can tell right in the middle of a page when he's had his first one.

↔ **Ernest Hemingway, according to Vladimir Nabokov**
I read him for the first time in the early forties, something about bells, balls, and bulls, and loathed it.

h. • Someone said that you are not fit to sleep with pigs. I stuck up for the

Catfight

↦ **Tom Wolfe, according to John Irving**

You see people reading him on airplanes, the same people who are reading John Grisham, for Christ's sake . . . I'm using the argument against him that he can't write, that his sentences are bad, that it makes you wince. You know, if you were a good skater, could you watch someone just fall down all the time? Could you do that? I can't do that.

↦ **Tom Wolfe, according to Norman Mailer**

At certain points, reading [*A Man in Full*] can even be said to resemble the act of making love to a three-hundred-pound woman. Once she gets on top, it's over. Fall in love, or be asphyxiated.

↦ **Tom Wolfe, according to John Updike**

A Man in Full still amounts to entertainment, not literature, even literature in a modest aspirant form. Like a movie desperate to recoup its bankers' investment, the novel tries too hard to please us.

↦ **John Irving, Norman Mailer, and John Updike, according to Tom Wolfe**

Larry, Curly, and Moe. Updike, Mailer, and Irving. My three stooges. . . . *A Man in Full* had frightened them. They were shaken. It was as simple as that. *A Man in Full* was an example . . . of the likely new direction: the intensely realistic novel . . . a revolution in content rather than form . . . that was about to sweep the arts in America, a revolution that would soon make many prestigious artists, such as our three old novelists, appear effete and irrelevant.

I will always love the false image I had of you.
—ASHLEIGH BRILLIANT

+++

She's so boring you fall asleep halfway through her name.
—ALAN BENNETT

++

She has been kissed as often as a police-court Bible, and by much the same class of people.
—ROBERTSON DAVIES

+++

Her skin was white as leprosy.
—S. T. COLERIDGE

++

He was about as useful in a crisis as a sheep.
—DOROTHY EDEN

++

I could never learn to like her, except on a raft at sea with no other provisions in sight.
—MARK TWAIN

He was trying to save both his faces.[27]

+++

That young girl is one of the least benightedly unintelligent organic life forms it has been my profound lack of pleasure not to be able to avoid meeting.

—DOUGLAS ADAMS

++

She looked like a huge ball of fur on two well-developed legs.

—NANCY MITFORD

+++

He was so crooked, you could have used his spine for a safety-pin.

—DOROTHY L. SAYERS

++

He is mad, bad, and dangerous to know.

—LADY CAROLINE LAMB

+++

She wears her clothes as if they were thrown on with a pitchfork.

—JONATHAN SWIFT

---

[27] Nowadays having "only" two faces would make him a paragon of nobility.

Dorothy Parker was invited to a party where most of the other guests looked as if they had stepped straight out of a church-hall production of La Bohème. "Where on earth do all these people come from?" her companion asked. "I think that after it's all over they crawl back into the woodwork," she replied.

~•~

She resembles the Venus de Milo: she is very old, has no teeth, and has white spots on her yellow skin.
—HEINRICH HEINE

••

Some people can stay longer in an hour than others can in a week.
—WILLIAM DEAN HOWELLS

•••

She not only expects the worst, but makes the worst of it when it happens.
—MICHAEL ARLEN

••

Failure has gone to his head.
—WILSON MIZNER

•••

Snarky Criticism

↔ An enthusiasm for Poe is the mark of a decidedly primitive stage of reflection.[28]

↔ Isn't she a poisonous thing of a woman, lying, concealing, flipping, plagiarising, misquoting, and being as clever a crooked literary publicist as ever?[29]

↔ I am reading Proust for the first time. Very poor stuff. I think he was mentally defective.[30]

↔ Every time I read *Pride and Prejudice*, I want to dig [Jane Austen] up and hit her over the skull with her own shin-bone.[31]

↔ E. M. Forster never gets any further than warming the teapot. He's a rare fine hand at that. Feel this teapot. Is it not beautifully warm? Yes, but there ain't going to be no tea.[32]

↔ I can't read ten pages of Steinbeck without throwing up.[33]

---

[28] Henry James on Edgar Allen Poe
[29] Dylan Thomas on Edith Sitwell
[30] Evelyn Waugh on Marcel Proust
[31] Mark Twain on Jane Austen
[32] Katherine Mansfield on E. M. Forster
[33] James Gould Cozzens on John Steinbeck

↝ His work is evil, and he is one of those unhappy beings of whom one can say that it would be better had he never been born.[34]

↝ A more sententious, holding-forth old bore, who expected every hero-worshipping adenoidal little twerp of a student-poet to hang on his every word I never saw.[35]

He is so mean, he won't let his little baby have more than one measle at a time.
—EUGENE FIELD

◆◆

Charles Lamb I sincerely believe to be in some considerable degree insane. A more pitiful, rickety, gasping, staggering, stammering tomfool I do not know. He is witty by denying truisms and abjuring good manners. His speech wriggles hither and thither with an incessant painful fluctuation; not an opinion in it or a fact or even a phrase that you can thank him for. . . .
—THOMAS CARLYLE

---

[34] Anatole France on Émile Zola
[35] James Dickey on Robert Frost

Bret Harte is a liar, a thief, a swindler, a snob, a sot, a sponge, a coward, a Jeremy Diddler, he is brim full of treachery, and he conceals his Jewish birth as carefully as if he considered it a disgrace.

—MARK TWAIN

✦✦✦

I regard you with an indifference bordering on aversion.

—ROBERT LOUIS STEVENSON

✦✦

She never lets ideas interrupt the easy flow of her conversation.

—JEAN WEBSTER

✦✦✦

God was bored by him.

—VICTOR HUGO

yourself couldn't have given you worse advice. ✦ Did your parents ever ask you t

SMARTS

(OR LACK THEREOF)

rom home? ◆ Do you want people to accept you as you are . . . or do you want them

SMARTS

OR LACK THEREOF

I'm exhausted. Knowing everything is hard work, and even though I kind of get off on maintaining my IQ while my fellow humans seem to be getting dumber than ever before, it's enough to make me take to my bed. Thank God you have this book in your hands—otherwise you might be tuning out to some idiotic reality television show or cruising porn on the 'Net. What's that? You want to jump in and say something? Here's some advice: Refrain from Twittering something that seems intellectual when you clearly don't know what you're talking about. If someone else's opinion is out there before yours . . . well, is that really so bad? Keep reading, pal. That's the only way to exercise your mind. You can be the sharpest knife in the drawer.[36]

The twinkle in his eyes is actually the sun shining between his ears.

You're changing your mind? And you think the new one will be any better?

Instant idiot. Just add alcohol.

I'm sorry, how many times did your parents drop you when you were a baby?

I am so clever sometimes I don't understand a single word of what I'm saying.

I'm sarcastic because it's the body's natural defense against stupid.

He's about as useless as the pope's testicles.

---

[36] Just remember that I'm a razor in comparison.

to like you? ✦ He has a mind like a steel trap—always closed. ✦ He is living proc

He's so stupid he got hit by a parked car.

✦

Does this rag smell like chloroform to you?

✦

You'd think such a little mind would be lonely in such a big head.

✦

If ignorance is bliss, you must be the happiest person alive.

✦

She doesn't know the meaning of the word "fear," but then again, she doesn't know the meaning of most words.

The IQ and the life expectancy of the average man recently passed each other in opposite directions.

Don't hesitate to speak your mind . . . you have nothing to lose.

How do you keep an idiot in suspense? Leave a message and I'll get back to you.

✦

Some people drink from the fountain of knowledge—it appears that you just gargled.

piss me off today, I'm running out of places to hide bodies. ✦ I have always wondere

Music, Drama, and Visual Art

Gee, what a terrific party. Later on we'll get some fluid and embalm each other.
—NEIL SIMON

AH, ARTISTS . . . PRIMA DONNAS, egotists, crybabies, horror shows, backstabbers, megalomaniacs. . . and those are the good ones. A good snarkist can always learn from these folks. They never hold back. Behold and marvel.

Nothing seems to give its participants the kind of carte blanche to behave any way they want more than the arts . . . as if being an "artist" is a passport to not having to obey the rules the rest of us mere mortals have to . . . so when they fight among themselves, sit back, grab a glass of your favorite libation, and let the games begin.

bang their heads against brick walls . . . then I met you.   •   Don't let your mind

What you said hurt me very much.
I cried all the way to the bank.
—LIBERACE

✦✦

He's a male chauvinistic piglet.
—BETTY FRIEDAN ON GROUCHO MARX

✦✦✦

If you really want to help the American theater,
darling, be an audience.
—TALLULAH BANKHEAD TO A YOUNG ACTRESS

✦✦

She had much in common with Hitler,
only no mustache.
—NOËL COWARD

~✦~

*When George Gershwin died in 1937, there
were many musical tributes written in praise of
the great composer. One of his fans persuaded
his friend, Oscar Levant, to hear his own
composition. Levant listened to the piece and
then told the proud composer: "I think it would
have been better if you had died and Gershwin
had written the elegy."*

~✦~

wander. It's way too small to be outside by itself. ✦ I had a nightmare. I dream

When you enter a room, you have to kiss his ring.
I don't mind, but he has it in his back pocket.
—DON RICKLES ON FRANK SINATRA

+++

Boy George is just what England needs—
another queen who can't dress.
—JOAN RIVERS

++

I had no idea Stravinsky disliked Debussy
as much as this.
—ERNEST NEWMAN, ON STRAVINSKY'S
SYMPHONY OF WIND INSTRUMENTS IN
MEMORY OF DEBUSSY

+++

I didn't like the play, but I saw it under adverse
conditions—the curtain was up.
—GEORGE S. KAUFMAN

++

He writes his plays for the ages—the
ages between five and twelve.
—GEORGE NATHAN ABOUT GEORGE BERNARD SHAW

+++

Her voice sounded like an eagle being goosed.
—RALPH NOVAK

Everyone is entitled to be stupid sometime, but you abuse the privilege. • I am

Shakespearean Insults[37]

↬ Thou detestable maw, thou womb of death.

↬ No longer from head to foot than from hip to hip, she is spherical, like a globe; I could find out countries in her.

↬ Thou lump of foul deformity.

↬ Thou unfit for any place but hell.

↬ He heareth not, he stirreth not, he moveth not, the ape is dead.

↬ You kiss by the book.

↬ Why, he's a man of wax.

↬ You should be women, and yet your beards forbid me to interpret that you are so.

↬ Whose horrible image doth unfix my hair and make my seated heart knock at my ribs.

↬ What you egg! You fry of treachery!

↬ Fit to govern! No, not to live.

---

[37] You may not understand them, but they certainly *sound* insulting.

↪ I had rather be a toad, and live upon the vapour of a dungeon, than keep a corner in the thing I love for others' uses.

↪ Damn her, lewd minx!

↪ You have such a February face, so full of frost, of storm and cloudiness.

↪ I do not like thy look, I promise thee.

↪ You Banbury cheese!

↪ Thou disease of a friend.

Critics? I love every bone in their heads.
—EUGENE O'NEILL

✦✦

The critic is often an unsuccessful author,
almost always an inferior one.
—LEIGH HUNT

✦✦✦

A drama critic is a man who knows the way
but can't drive the car.
—KENNETH TYNAN

Match the Insult to the Show[38]

A. *Guys and Dolls*   D. *Gypsy*
B. *Glengarry Glen Ross*   E. *Romeo and Juliet*
C. *West Side Story*   F. *Come Back, Little Sheba*

~✦~

1. Thy head is as full of quarrels as an egg is full of meat.
2. Why don't you get smart, you stupid hooligans? I oughta take you down to the station and throw you in the can right now. You and the tin-horn immigrant scum you come from.
3. I kinda like it when you forget to give me presents. It makes me feel like we're married.
4. You're like a pioneer woman without a frontier.
5. Alcoholics are mostly disappointed men.
6. Cop couldn't find his fucking couch in the living room.

Who picks your clothes—Stevie Wonder?
—DON RICKLES TO FRANK SINATRA

✦✦

He has plenty of music in him, but he cannot get it out.
—ALFRED, LORD TENNYSON ON ROBERT BROWNING

---

[38] 1. E., 2. C., 3. A., 4. D., 5. F., 6. B.

time I wanted somebody's fingers to break so badly. ✦ Cancel my subscriptions. .

A medical student was in the morgue one day after classes, getting a little practice in before the final exams. He went over to a table where a body was lying facedown. He removed the sheet from the body and found a cork in the corpse's rectum. He pulled the cork out, and to his surprise, music began playing: "On the road again . . . Just can't wait to get on the road again . . ." The student replaced the cork immediately, and the music stopped. He did it again. Same thing. Totally freaked out, he called the medical examiner over to the corpse.

He pulled the cork back out again and the music started. He looked up at the man, expecting him to be shocked. "Isn't that the wildest thing you've ever seen?"

"So what?" the medical examiner replied, obviously unimpressed with the student's discovery. "Any asshole can sing country music."

~♦~

To me, the *Mona Lisa* looks like she's chewing toffee.
—JUSTIN MOORHOUSE

Insults and More Insults

↔ Anton Bruckner wrote the same symphony nine times (ten actually), trying to get it right. He failed.[39]

↔ He is the only genius with an IQ of 60.[40]

↔ If I found her floating in my pool, I'd punish my dog.[41]

↔ As for Cézanne, his name will be forever linked with the most memorable artistic joke of the last fifteen years.[42]

↔ Watching your performance from the rear of the house. Wish you were here.[43]

↔ It is bad when they don't perform your operas—but when they do, it's far worse.[44]

---

[39] Edward Abbey on Anton Bruckner
[40] Gore Vidal talking about Andy Warhol
[41] Joan Rivers on Yoko Ono
[42] Camille Mauclair on Paul Cézanne
[43] George S. Kaufman to actor William Gaxton
[44] Camille Saint-Saens on Dame Ethel Smyth

↔ Listening to the Fifth Symphony of Ralph Vaughan Williams is like staring at a cow for forty-five minutes.[45]

↔ It resembles a tortoiseshell cat having a fit in a plate of tomatoes.[46]

His pictures seem to resemble not pictures but a sample book of patterns of linoleum.
—CYRIL ASQUITH ON PAUL KLEE

✦✦✦

I have seen, and heard, much of Cockney impudence before now; but never expected to hear a coxcomb ask two hundred guineas for flinging a pot of paint in the public's face.
—JOHN RUSKIN ON JAMES McNEIL WHISTLER

✦✦

A decorator tainted with insanity.
—KENYON COX ON PAUL GAUGUIN

✦✦✦

He's a mental midget
with the IQ of a fence post.
—TOM WAITS

---

[45] Aaron Copland on Ralph Vaughan Williams
[46] Mark Twain on J. M. W. Turner's *The Slave Ship*

On Wagner

Wagner has beautiful moments but awful quarter hours.
—GIOVANNI ROSSINI

++

I like Wagner's music better than any other music. It is so loud that one can talk the whole time without people hearing what one says. That is a great advantage.
—OSCAR WILDE

+++

Is Wagner actually a man? Is he not rather a disease? Everything he touches falls ill: he has made music sick.
—FRIEDRICH WILHELM NIETZSCHE

++

I can't listen to that much Wagner. I start getting the urge to conquer Poland.
—WOODY ALLEN

+++

Wagner's music is better than it sounds.
—MARK TWAIN

I feel the same way about disco as I do about herpes.
—THE EDGE

and a little more shut the hell up? • Let's see, I've walked the dog, cleaned my room,

I liked your opera. I think I will set it to music.
—LUDWIG VAN BEETHOVEN TO A FELLOW COMPOSER

++

The trouble with her is that she lacks the power of
conversation but not the power of speech.
—GEORGE BERNARD SHAW

+++

The only thing Madonna will ever do like a virgin
is give birth in a stable.
—BETTE MIDLER

++

He's so annoying he makes me want to rip my eyeballs out
just to have something to plug my ears with.

+++

You know, if you play the Jonas Brothers backward . . . they
still suck. But it gives 'em an edge.

++

They found a new chamber in the Great Pyramid. And
here's what was on the wall: Rolling Stones Tour, 1567 BC.
—CRAIG KILBORN

+++

The Rolling Stones' new U.S. tour is a lot harder than their
first, when we only had thirteen states.
—JAY LENO

bing, and gossiped with my friends . . . nope, this list doesn't say that I'm required to

Snarkin' the News

↪ The Vatican has stated that they forgive the Beatles. For what, you ask? For the Jesus remark, for inciting young girls to a sexual frenzy, and for firing Pete Best.

↪ Carly Simon has revealed, after thirty-eight years, that the subject of "You're So Vain" was David Geffen. She's re-recording the song, changing the lyrics to: "I'm so vain, I bet I think people still care."

↪ Lil Wayne was sent to Rikers for gun possession. I have the number fifteen in the betting pool, based on how many times he hears the word "lollipop" on a daily basis until he's out.

↪ Snoop Dogg has been trying to end his ban to play in England. Originally barred for using "insulting words," the Snoop camp maintains that the Brits just don't understand that "suck my izzle" is not derogatory.

↪ Tiny Tim's ex-manager is trying to open an 8-track museum, claiming this is a format that should never be forgotten. There will be four entry ways that may or may not get you where you wanna go and an AMC Pacer will be permanently parked in front.

talk to you. ✦ The village just called. They said they were missing their idiot. I cou

↔ They've opened ABBAWORLD in London. It's 30,000 square feet and has a gift shop full of ABBA memorabilia and ABBA songs playing on a loop in every room. There's even a 3-D holographic ABBA that visitors can pretend to perform with. What's Swedish for "please kill me"?

So you're acting now, you're in a vampire movie, yes? That's good. Finally, a role that *requires* you to suck.
—TRIUMPH THE INSULT COMIC DOG TO BON JOVI

~+~

Q. What's the difference between God and Bono?

A. God doesn't walk around thinking he's Bono.

~+~

A freakish homunculus germinated
outside of lawful procreation.
—HENRY ARTHUR JONES ON GEORGE BERNARD SHAW

understand them, but I'm pretty sure they were saying your name. ◆ Of course I'd

More Shakespearean Insults

- ↔ Your means are very slender, and your waste is great.

- ↔ You are as a candle, the better part burnt out.

- ↔ I think he be transformed into a beast, for I can nowhere find him like a man.

- ↔ Away! Thou art poison to my blood.

- ↔ As I told you always, her beauty and her brain go not together.

- ↔ I'll pray a thousand prayers for thy death.

- ↔ Come, you are a tedious fool.

- ↔ Were I like thee, I would throw away myself.

- ↔ Would thou wert clean enough to spit upon!

- ↔ I'll beat thee, but I should infect my hands.

- ↔ Thou art like the harpy, which, to betray, dost with thine angels face, seize with thine eagle's talons.

- ↔ Your peevish chastity, which is not worth a breakfast in the cheapest country.

- ↔ He is open to incontinency.

- ↔ A knot you are of damned blood-suckers.

↪ Thy mother's name is ominous to children.

↪ Pray you, stand farther from me!

↪ You blocks, you stones, you worse than senseless things!

↪ There's many a man hath more hair than wit.

↪ If thou art chang'd to aught, tis to an ass.

He's liked, but he's not well liked.
—ARTHUR MILLER

✦✦

No one can have a higher opinion of him than I have; and I think he's a dirty little beast.
—W. S. GILBERT

✦✦✦

You know what charm is: a way of getting the answer yes without having asked any clear question.
—ALBERT CAMUS

✦✦

He was so narrow-minded that if he fell on a pin it would blind him in both eyes.
—FRED ALLEN

but I can't seem to get my head that far up my ass. ✦ Mirrors don't talk . . . but,

I hate journalists. There is nothing in them but tittering jeering emptiness. They have all made what Dante calls the Great Refusal. . . . The shallowest people on the ridge of the earth.

—WILLIAM BUTLER YEATS

~♦~

George Bernard Shaw answered a knock at his door one day and was greeted by a couple who announced gravely: "Good morning, we are Jehovah's Witnesses." "Good morning," said Shaw, "I'm Jehovah. How are we doing?"

~♦~

Man is a useless passion.

—JEAN-PAUL SARTRE

♦♦♦

He's completely unspoiled by failure.

—NOËL COWARD

♦♦

We are all born mad. Some remain so.

—SAMUEL BECKETT

lucky for you, they don't laugh, either. ♦ He's got diarrhea of the mouth and const

~+~

The great nineteenth-century Shakespearean director Sir Henry Irving visited the American actor Richard Mansfield, immediately after his performance as Richard III, which Irving had never seen before. He found Mansfield in his dressing room, running with sweat after his exertions onstage, and, patting him on the shoulder, Irving said: "Well, Dick, me boy! I see your skin acts well."

~+~

your breath. . . . You'll need it to blow up your date. ✦ People clap when they see

Movies, Television, and Actors

> You had to stand in line to hate him.
> —HEDDA HOPPER

AH YES, SHOW BUSINESS. There's no business like it, so the song goes. . . . and there's no other group of folks where the snark reigns supreme. Figures, no? What else do overpaid, overpampered, overindulged people have to do with their time than engage in one on ones with others of their kind? I know it works for me.

This section includes the crème de la crème of the snark ideology, folks like Mae West and Groucho Marx and W. C. Fields and many more. Like the "no animals were harmed in the making of this film" all-inclusive pardon at the end of every movie, no punches were pulled in the making of this chapter.

Match the Insult to the Movie[47]

A. *Christmas Vacation*   D. *Dazed and Confused*
B. *The Ref*   E. *The Departed*
C. *The Big Sleep*   F. *Garden State*

~•~

1. I'm the guy that does his job. You must be the other guy.
2. My, my, my. So many guns around town and so few brains.
3. What are you looking at? Wipe that face off your head, bitch.
4. Can I refill your eggnog for you? Get you something to eat? Drive you out to the middle of nowhere and leave you for dead?
5. If there was a retarded Oscar you would win, hands down.
6. You know what I'm going to get you next Christmas, Mom? A big wooden cross, so that every time you feel unappreciated for your sacrifices, you can climb on up and nail yourself to it.

---

[47] 1. E., 2. C., 3. D., 4. A., 5. F., 6. B.

Is that your nose, or did a bus
park on your face?
—*ROXANNE*

♦♦♦

She's been on more laps than a napkin.
—WALTER WINCHELL

♦♦

There's nothing wrong with you that
reincarnation won't cure.[48]
—JACK E. LEONARD

♦♦♦

If I wanted to talk to an asshole,
I would have farted.
—ANDREW DICE CLAY

♦♦

To call you stupid would be an insult to stupid people!
I've known sheep who could outwit you.
I've worn dresses with higher IQs, but you
think you're an intellectual, don't you, ape?
—*A FISH CALLED WANDA*

---

[48] [If I were reincarnated . . .] I'd come back as my wife and leave
me the hell alone.—Jeff Dunham

Snarkin' the News

↪ A monkey in a Russian zoo, fed vodka and ciga-
rettes by tourists, was diagnosed as alcoholic and
nicotine addicted. He has been placed in rehab, suffering from "exhaustion." No comment was forthcoming from his roommate, Charlie Sheen.

↪ Right out of a WB cartoon: A man in New Jersey
was standing on a corner when a piano that was
being lowered from the third story of a building fell,
killing him instantly. The piano landed upright and
was completely unharmed.

↪ Mattel is coming out with a set of *Mad Men* Barbie
dolls, complete with fedoras, sharkskin suits, and
bad cocktail dresses. Infidelity, guilt, and repression
sold separately.

You're a parasite for sore eyes.
—GREGORY RATOFF

♦♦

Hitler got more laughs than Jimmy Kimmel, and he did it
without Jewish writers.
—LISA LAMPANELLI

more comfortable . . . like a coma? • Go outside and play "Hide and go f**k yourself."

If people don't sit at Chaplin's feet, he goes out and stands
where they are sitting.
—HERMAN J. MANKIEWICZ

~✦~

*Peter Lorre: "You despise me, don't you?"
Humphrey Bogart: "If I gave you any thought,
I probably would."*

—*CASABLANCA*

~✦~

Next time I see you, remind me not to talk to you.
—GROUCHO MARX

✦✦✦

Why are we honoring this man? Have we
run out of human beings?
—MILTON BERLE

✦✦

They used to photograph Shirley Temple through gauze.
They should photograph me through linoleum.
—TALLULAH BANKHEAD

She has the attention span of a lightning bolt.
—ROBERT REDFORD

✦✦✦

Insults and More Insults

↔ He's the type of man who will end up dying in his own arms.[49]

↔ He couldn't ad-lib a fart after a baked-bean dinner.[50]

↔ He looked like a half-melted rubber bulldog.[51]

↔ His ears made him look like a taxicab with both doors open.[52]

↔ He is to acting what Liberace is to pumping iron.[53]

↔ Her body has gone to her head.[54]

---

[49] Mamie Van Doren about Warren Beatty
[50] Johnny Carson about Chevy Chase
[51] John Simon on Walter Matthau
[52] Howard Hughes about Clark Gable
[53] Rex Reed on Sylvester Stallone
[54] Barbara Stanwyck about Marilyn Monroe

She has discovered the secret of
perpetual middle age.
—OSCAR LEVANT

◆◆

He has a Teflon brain . . . nothing sticks.
—LILY TOMLIN

◆◆◆

She looked as though butter wouldn't melt in her
mouth—or anywhere else.
—ELSA LANCHESTER

~◆~

*Geena Davis: "Don't put it there! It'll make a
bulge. People can see!" Samuel Jackson: "Want
me to put it in my pants and shoot my damn
dick off?" Geena Davis: "Now you're a sharp-
shooter?"*

—*LONG KISS GOODNIGHT*

~◆~

Her figure described a set of parabolas that could cause
cardiac arrest in a yak.
—WOODY ALLEN

Her only flair is in her nostrils.
—PAULINE KAEL

••

He hasn't an enemy in the world—but
all his friends hate him.
—EDDIE CANTOR

•••

Mae West

↔ When it comes to men, she never turns down anything except the bedcovers.

↔ She's the kind of woman who climbed the ladder of
success—wrong by wrong.

↔ He's the kind of man who picks his friends—to
pieces.

↔ She's the finest woman that ever walked the streets.

↔ His mother should have thrown him away and kept
the stork.

I treasure every moment I don't see her.
—OSCAR LEVANT ON PHYLLIS DILLER

with your IQ should have a low voice, too. • A half-wit gave you a piece of his mind

She has breasts of granite and a mind like a Gruyere cheese.
—BILLY WILDER ABOUT MARILYN MONROE

◆◆

She was a master at making nothing happen very slowly.
—CLIFTON FADIMAN

◆◆◆

You look into his eyes, and you get the feeling
someone else is driving.
—DAVID LETTERMAN

◆◆

If you die horribly on television, you will not have died in
vain. You will have entertained us.
—KURT VONNEGUT

◆◆◆

The best part of you ran down your mother's leg.
—JACKIE GLEASON

~◆~

*Lucille: "Oh, please. I've been drinking since
before you were born. So if alcohol's the reason
I'm here, I got news for you, Bub. It's the only
reason you're here, too." Michael: "Hey, look at
that. You're mean sober, too."*

—*ARRESTED DEVELOPMENT*

~◆~

ld on to it. ◆ A sharp tongue is no indication of a keen mind. ◆ Alone: In bad

Snarkin' the News

↔ A group of doctors are asking the hot dog industry to change the shape of the fast food to help prevent choking accidents. Another possible solution was to make them all twelve inches or longer. Jenna Jameson could not be located to comment.

↔ "It's a docusoap, not a reality show." So says socialite Julie Kirby of the TV show *High Society*, claiming the producers edited it "to make me look like a stupid bitch." They also edited it to make it look like she can chew gum, walk, and scream at people simultaneously.

↔ Jessica Simpson almost cried recently on *Oprah*, recalling the story of meeting a model in France who had withered down to sixty-two pounds. She said "it made me very emotional." Asked how she stays in shape, she replied that she is currently on the French Model Diet.

↔ There has been protest over a forthcoming John F. Kennedy miniseries from a creator of *24*. Protesters claim it's a right-wing character assassination and completely manufactured. This is based on an early screening of the film where JFK is shown having a three-way with Lady Gaga and Beyoncé.

↝ It's been reported Charlie Sheen has left his hit TV show . . . to do what? Shakespeare in the Park? *Two and a Half Gentlemen of Verona?*

He has the mathematical abilities of a Clydesdale.
—DAVID LETTERMAN

✦✦

Is Elizabeth Taylor fat? Her favorite food is seconds.
—JOAN RIVERS

✦✦✦

What's on your mind? If you'll forgive the overstatement.
—FRED ALLEN

~✦~

A friendly old vicar met Groucho Marx for the first time and started to tell him how much he enjoyed his films. "I want to thank you Mr. Marx for all the enjoyment you've given the world," he said. "And I want to thank you for all the enjoyment you've taken out of it," replied Groucho.

~✦~

nd of yours. ✦ As useless as rubber lips on a woodpecker. ✦ Don't mind him. He

Groucho Marx

↔ He may look like an idiot and talk like an idiot, but don't let that fool you. He really is an idiot.

↔ I'll bet your father spent the first year of your life throwing rocks at the stork.

↔ Why don't you bore a hole in yourself and let the sap run out?

↔ You've got the brain of a four-year-old boy, and I bet he was glad to get rid of it.

↔ I never forget a face, but in your case I'll make an exception.

↔ I have nothing but confidence in you . . . and very little of that.

↔ I could dance with you until the cows come home . . . on second thought, I'd rather dance with the cows until you come home.

↔ Don't look now, but there's one man too many in this room, and I think it's you.

↔ I can see you in the kitchen, bending over a hot stove . . . but I can't see the stove.

↦ She got her good looks from her father. He's a plastic surgeon.

↦ Now there goes a man with an open mind. You can feel the draft from here.

When you go to the mind reader, do you get half price?
—DAVID LETTERMAN

✦✦

She doesn't understand the concept of
Roman numerals. She thinks we fought
in World War Eleven.
—JOAN RIVERS

✦✦✦

If at first you don't succeed,
keep on suckin' til you do suck seed.
—CURLY (OF THE THREE STOOGES)

✦✦

In order to feel safe on his private jet, John
Travolta purchased a bomb-sniffing dog.
The dog came six movies too late.
—TINA FEY

the privilege. ✦ It's an excellent time to become a missing person. ✦ Fat? You're

Catfight

↪ I wouldn't piss on her if she was on fire.
—Bette Davis on Joan Crawford

↪ Take away the pop eyes, the cigarette, and those funny clipped words, and what have you got? She's phony, but I guess the public likes that.
—Joan Crawford on Bette Davis

↪ The best time I ever had with Joan Crawford was when I pushed her down the stairs in *Whatever Happened to Baby Jane?* —Bette Davis

↪ Why am I so good at playing bitches? I think it's because I'm not a bitch. Maybe that's why Miss Crawford always plays ladies. —Bette Davis

↪ I didn't know her well, but after watching her in action I didn't want to know her well.
—Joan Crawford on Bette Davis

↪ There goes the famous good time that was had by all. —Bette Davis on Joan Crawford

↪ Miss Davis was always partial to covering up her face in motion pictures. She called it "art." Others might call it camouflage—a cover-up for the absence of any real beauty. —Joan Crawford

Critics are eunuchs at a gang bang.
—GEORGE BURNS

♦♦

Brassy, brazen witch on a mortgaged broomstick,
a steamroller with cleats.
—WALTER KERR ON ETHEL MERMAN

♦♦♦

I have more talent in my smallest
fart than you have in your entire body.
—WALTER MATTHAU

♦♦

He had a winning smile, but everything else
was a loser.
—GEORGE C. SCOTT

~♦~

*W. C. Fields, when asked why he never drank
water, replied, "Fish fuck in it."*

~♦~

Of course we all know that Morris was a wonderful
all-round man, but the act of walking round him
has always tired me.
—MAX BEERBOHM ON WILLIAM MORRIS

♦ Grasp your ears firmly and remove your head from your ass. ♦ He has the IQ

You tweachewous miscweant!
—ELMER FUDD

+++

She's descended from a long line her
mother listened to.
—GYPSY ROSE LEE

~+~

*Triumph the Insult Comic Dog at a movie
opening: "Okay, it's time for Star Wars trivia.
First question: 'What substance was Han Solo
frozen in?'" Crowd: "Carbonite!" Triumph:
"No no, I'm sorry, I'm very sorry, the correct
answer is 'Who gives a shit?'"*

~+~

In California, they don't throw their garbage away—
they make it into TV shows.
—WOODY ALLEN

++

Kirstie Alley says she makes her new boyfriends wait six
months to have sex with her. Of course, some insist on
twelve months.
—CONAN O'BRIEN

of lint. • Have you considered suing your brains for nonsupport? • He can o

I'd call him a sadistic, hippophilic necrophile, but that would be beating a dead horse.
—WOODY ALLEN

+++

She has a face that belongs to the sea and the wind, with large rocking-horse nostrils and teeth that you just know bite an apple every day.
—CECIL BEATON ABOUT KATHARINE HEPBURN

++

He has turned almost alarmingly blond—he's gone past platinum, he must be plutonium; his hair is coordinated with his teeth.
—PAULINE KAEL ABOUT ROBERT REDFORD

+++

Roman Polanski is a four-foot Pole you wouldn't want to touch with a ten-foot pole.[55]
—KENNETH TYNAN

++

It's a new low for actresses when you have to wonder what's between her ears instead of her legs.
—KATHERINE HEPBURN ABOUT SHARON STONE

---

[55] That's not to say he wouldn't touch you if you were a thirteen-year-old girl.

ith that nose! ✦ He comes from a long line of real estate people . . . they're a vacant

Match the Insult to the Sitcom[56]

A. *The Office*
(Dwight Schrute)

B. *Roseanne*
(Roseanne)

C. *The Muppet Show*
(Statler and Waldorf)

D. *Curb Your Enthusiasm*
(Larry David)

E. *The Simpsons*
(Groundskeeper Willie)

F. *Family Guy*
(Stewie Griffin)

~♦~

1. Well, I'd love to stay and chat, but you're a total bitch.
2. Bonjour, you cheese-eating surrender-monkeys!
3. Switzerland is a place where they don't like to fight, so they get people to do their fighting for them while they ski and eat chocolate.
4. Dolphins get a lot of good publicity for the drowning swimmers they push back to shore, but what you don't hear about is the many people they push farther out to sea! Dolphins aren't smart. They just like pushing things.
5. Your idea of romance is popping the can away from my face.
6. Wake up, you old fool, you slept through the show. Who's a fool? You watched it.

---

[56] 1. F., 2. E., 3. D., 4. A., 5. B., 6. C .

BEAUTY

(OR LACK THEREOF)

He just forgot to wind it up this morning. ✦ He has depth, but only on the surface.

BEAUTY

(OR LACK THEREOF)

You know that not particularly clever phrase "coyote ugly"? Meaning that you wake up with the person you met in the bar last night when you were so drunk that you actually thought you looked good in the bathroom mirror[57] and this person is laying on your arm and you'd almost rather chew it off than wake them . . . you don't want to get there. I realize that looks are subjective . . . just please don't subject me to the bad ones. I've heard some wise men claim that confidence makes up for ugliness, but I dunno, it doesn't work for me. Makeup can go a ways to help, and being generous sexually is always a good remedy—some faces look a lot better from the top of the head down. Be careful, though . . . it's actually harder to run with just one arm.

Do you think that I'll lose my looks when I get older? With luck, yes . . .

•

Roses are red, violets are blue, God made me pretty; what the hell happened to you?

You used to look your age; now, you don't even look your species.

•

Your hairdresser must really hate you.

•

He has the face of a saint—a Saint Bernard.

Hit with the ugly stick? You must have been born in the ugly forest. Looks like you fell out of the ugly tree and hit every branch on the way down.

---

[57] Even though the shiny part had actually peeled off.

When you come into a room, the mice jump on chairs.

✦

Well, obviously this day was a total waste of makeup.

✦

I always say that the best years of a woman's life are the ten years between thirty and thirty-one.

✦

You're lucky to be born beautiful; unlike me, who was born a huge liar.

That woman's had her face lifted so many times there's nothing left inside her shoes.

You look like you comb your hair with an eggbeater.

✦

See, that's what's meant by dark and handsome. When it's dark, he's handsome.

Don't hate me because I'm beautiful . . . hate me because your boyfriend thinks I'm beautiful.

e brain cell, and it is fighting for dominance. ✦ He is so short his hair smells like

feet ✦ He is the kind of a man that you would use as a blueprint to build an idiot.

Politics and Current Events

What's the difference between a Democrat and a
Republican? A Democrat blows, a Republican sucks.
—LEWIS BLACK

YOU'RE NOT REALLY SUPPOSED to discuss
politics in anyone's company. One could reasonably
argue that the whole process is one big insult. Republicans
hate the Democrats, Democrats hate the Republicans (and
themselves) . . . You take one side, he'll take another, throw in
yet a third, and let the battle commence. Nothing brings out
the need to insult more than people's political views.

the street he owned after his wife. What a grand statement of his love for her. She

Roosevelt proved that a man could be president for life,
Truman proved that anybody could be president, and
Eisenhower proved we don't need to have a president.
—KENNETH B. KEATING

++

He was so narrow-minded he could see through a keyhole
with both eyes.
—MOLLY IVINS

+++

Use of the Word "Fuck" in History

"What the fuck was that?"
Mayor of Hiroshima

"Where the fuck is all this water coming from?"
Captain of the *Titanic*

"That's not a real fucking gun."
John Lennon

"Who's gonna fucking find out?"
Richard Nixon

"Heads are going to fucking roll."
Anne Boleyn

"Any fucking idiot could understand that."
Albert Einstein

was cold, hard, cracked, and only got plowed around the holidays.   •   He smells the

"It does so fucking look like her!"
Picasso

"How the fuck did you work that out?"
Pythagoras

"You want what on the fucking ceiling?"
Michaelangelo

"Fuck a duck."
Walt Disney

"Why? Because it's fucking there!"
Edmund Hillary

"I don't suppose it's gonna fucking rain?"
Joan of Arc

"Scattered fucking showers my ass."
Noah

"I need this parade like I need a fucking hole in my head."
John F. Kennedy

He has every attribute of a dog except loyalty.
—THOMAS P. GORE

n't find the pot. • He would be out of his depth in a parking-lot puddle. • He'd

Why hate someone for the color of their skin when there are
much better reasons to hate them? Racism isn't born, folks,
it's taught. I have a two-year-old son. You know what he
hates? Naps! End of list.

—DENIS LEARY

Insults and More Insults

↔ You really have to get to know him to dislike him.[58]

↔ A triumph of the embalmer's art.[59]

↔ Attila the Hen.[60]

↔ She loves nature—in spite of what it did to her.[61]

↔ He looks as though he's been weaned on a pickle.[62]

↔ He can't help it—he was born with a silver foot in
his mouth.[63]

↔ His mind was like a soup dish, wide and shallow;
it could hold a small amount of nearly anything,

---

[58] James T. Patterson on Thomas Dewey
[59] Gore Vidal on Ronald Reagan
[60] Clement Freud on Margaret Thatcher
[61] Bette Midler on a member of the Royal Family
[62] Alice Roosevelt Longworth on Calvin Coolidge
[63] Ann Richards on George Bush

steal the straw from his mother's kennel. • He's got that faraway look. The farthe

but the slightest jarring spilled the soup into some-body's lap.[64]

↔ Why, this fellow don't know any more about poli-tics than a pig knows about Sunday.[65]

↔ He has the lucidity which is the by-product of a fundamentally sterile mind.[66]

Little things affect little minds.
—BENJAMIN DISRAELI

~+~

When he was a young reporter, the journalist Heywood Broun was sent to interview a very stuffy member of Congress on a very controversial subject. "I have nothing to say, young man," said the Congressman haughtily. "I know," said Broun, "now shall we get on with the interview?"

~+~

---

[64] Irving Stone on William Jennings Bryan
[65] Harry S. Truman about Dwight D. Eisenhower
[66] Aneurin Bevan about Neville Chamberlain

the better he looks. ◆ He's not stupid; he's possessed by a retarded ghost. ◆ He's

He has no more backbone than a chocolate éclair.

—THEODORE ROOSEVELT

♦♦

His ignorance is encyclopedic.

—ABBA EBAN

♦♦♦

If he were any dumber, he'd be a tree.

—BARRY GOLDWATER

♦♦

He could never see a belt without hitting below it.

—MARGOT ASQUITH

♦♦♦

He never said a foolish thing nor ever did a wise one.

—EARL OF ROCHESTER

♦♦

The higher a monkey climbs, the more you see of its behind.

—JOSEPH STILWELL

♦♦♦

The nine most terrifying words in the English language are
"I'm from the government and I'm here to help."

—RONALD REAGAN

♦♦

Condoleezza Rice is sexy in sort of an ice-cold praying
mantis sort of way.

—STEPHEN COLBERT

so dense that light bends around him. ♦ He's the first in his family born wi

~♦~

Bessie Braddock to Churchill: "Winston, you're drunk!" Churchill: "Bessie, you're ugly, but tomorrow morning I shall be sober."

~♦~

He was as great as a man can be without morality.[67]
—ALEXIS DE TOCQUEVILLE

♦♦♦

Yeah, we're friends. Like Hitler and Mussolini.

♦♦

She spends her day powdering her face till
she looks like a bled pig.
—MARGOT ASQUITH

♦♦♦

He strains his conversation through a cigar.
—HAMILTON MABIE

♦♦

U2 lead singer Bono met with President Bush at the White House. Bono urged the President to help the world's poor. Bush urged Bono to get back with Cher.
—TINA FEY

---

[67] No, this *isn't* a compliment meant for politicians!

He's the only man who, if told to screw himself, could do it. ♦ He's the reason

Match the Insult to the Politician[68]

A. Abraham Lincoln   D. Winston Churchill
B. Henry Clay   E. Henry Kissinger
C. Margaret Thatcher   F. Thomas Jefferson

~♦~

1. They are not fit to manage a whelk stall.
2. Ninety percent of the politicians give the other ten percent a bad name.
3. He is ignorant, passionate, hypocritical, corrupt; and easily swayed by the basest men who surround him.
4. If I could not go to heaven but with a party, I would not go there at all.
5. Whenever I hear anyone arguing for slavery, I feel a strong impulse to see it tried on him personally.
6. In politics if you want anything said, ask a man. If you want anything done, ask a woman.

I believe that Ronald Reagan can make this country what it once was—an Arctic region covered with ice.
—STEVE MARTIN

---

[68] 1. D., 2. E., 3. B., 4. F., 5. A., 6. C.

brothers and sisters shouldn't marry. ♦ His brain waves fall a little short

~•~

A man was walking in the woods and came to a cottage where the walls were covered with clocks. He asked the woman who owned the cottage what all the clocks were for. She replied that everyone in the world had a clock, and every time you told a lie your clock advanced a second. He saw a clock that was hardly moving, and when he remarked about it he was told that it was Mother Teresa's. He then asked where Bill Clinton's clock was. The woman replied, "It's in the kitchen—we're using it as a ceiling fan."

~•~

He is nothing more than a well-meaning baboon.
—GENERAL GEORGE McCLELLAN
ON ABRAHAM LINCOLN

•••

He was distinguished for ignorance; for he had only one idea and that was wrong.
—BENJAMIN DISRAELI

••

He can compress the most words into the smallest idea of any man I know.
—ABRAHAM LINCOLN

• His men would follow him anywhere but only out of morbid curiosity. • His

Snarkin' the News

↔ Virginia state delegate Bob Marshall stated recently that "kids born . . . with handicaps" are God's revenge for an earlier abortion. I'm thinking he's God's revenge for evolution.

↔ A North Carolina Congressman is trying to replace Grant on the $50 bill with Ronald Reagan. He has support, but, if it passes, it would mean that you could only spend it on the military or give it to huge corporations.

↔ U.S. Representative Eric Massa resigned recently, and his male coworkers are just tickled pink about it. Word was he was quite hard on the members of his staff.

↔ Iran claims it now has uranium with 20 percent purity, to which the White House has responded, "No you don't." . . . Acting WMD assessor Stevie Wonder confirmed that position.

↔ Sarah Palin was recently hired to do FOX News. In a related story, Natasha and Boris were hired to do Moose and Squirrel news.

origins are so low, you'd have to limbo under his family tree. • His personality's

↔ The Germans have developed a technology that steers a car according to where the driver's eyes are looking. Keep that away from Congress or the women of Washington are doomed.

↔ More military news: An eight-year-old boy was drafted into the Ukrainian army. His parents alerted the authorities but the boy was still required to show up at the conscription center. After taking the intelligence test, they made him a colonel.

If you're so pro-life, do me a favor: don't lock arms and block medical clinics. If you're so pro-life, lock arms and block cemeteries.
—BILL HICKS

✦✦✦

He knows nothing and thinks he knows everything. That points clearly to a political career.
—GEORGE BERNARD SHAW

✦✦

Bill Clinton's foreign policy experience is pretty much confined to having had breakfast once at the International House of Pancakes.
—PAT BUCHANAN

ways he goes alone for group therapy. ✦ I believe in respect for the dead; in fact I

The cruelest thing that has happened to
Lincoln since he was shot by Booth was to fall
into the hands of Carl Sandburg.
—EDMUND WILSON

~✦~

*The Earl of Sandwich told John Wilkes, "You,
Mr. Wilkes, will die either of the pox or on the
gallows." Wilkes's response: "That depends, my
lord, whether I embrace your mistress or your
principles."*

~✦~

A sophisticated rhetorician, inebriated with the
exuberance of his own verbosity.
—BENJAMIN DISRAELI

✦✦✦

Republicans are so empty-headed, they wouldn't make a
good landfill.
—JIM HIGHTOWER

✦✦

He has sat on the fence so long that the iron has
entered his soul.
—DAVID LLOYD GEORGE

could only respect you if you *were* dead. ✦ I bet your brain feels as good as new,

Winston Churchill

- ↔ He has all the virtues I dislike and none of the vices I admire.

- ↔ He's a sheep in sheep's clothing.

- ↔ He's a modest little person, with much to be modest about.

- ↔ There but for the grace of God, goes God.

Well, I think we ought to let him hang there.
Let him twist slowly, slowly in the wind.
—JOHN EHRLICHMAN ON JOHN DEAN[69]

♦♦♦

His smile is like the silver plate on a coffin.
—JOHN PHILPOT CURRAN

♦♦

They never open their mouths without subtracting from the
sum of human knowledge.
—THOMAS BRACKETT REED

---

[69] So thought Haldeman about Liddy, Liddy about Dean, and
Dean about Ehrlichman . . . and around it goes.

~+~

A woman is driving along when the car in front of her hits the brakes suddenly, and she plows into it. An extremely short man gets out, looks at the damage, and says, "I'm not happy . . ." "Well, which one are you?" the woman replies.

~+~

Being attacked by him is like being savaged by a dead sheep.
—DENNIS HEALY

+++

Cop Snark

↭ I can't reach my license unless you hold my beer.

↭ Sorry, Officer, I didn't realize my radar detector wasn't plugged in.

↭ Aren't you that guy from the Village People?

↭ Hey, you must have been doin' at least 120 mph to keep up with me . . . Good job!

↭ Excuse me . . . is "stick up" hyphenated?

↭ I almost decided to be a cop, but I decided to finish high school instead.

↭ Bad cop! No doughnut!

years? ✦ Was your brother an only child? ✦ He went to have his head examined, t

↔ You're not gonna check the trunk, are you?

↔ Didn't I see you get your ass kicked on *Cops*?

↔ Is it true that people become cops because they're too dumb to work at McDonald's?

↔ So, uh, you on the take, or what?

↔ I was trying to keep up with traffic. Yes, I know there are no other cars around—that's how far ahead of me they are.

↔ What do you mean, "Have I been drinking?" You're the trained specialist.

↔ Hey, can you give me another one of those full cavity searches?

Americans have different ways of saying things; they say "elevator," we say "lift"; they say "President," we say "stupid psychopathic git."
—ALEXEI SAYLE

++

A four-hundred-dollar suit on him would look like socks on a rooster.
—EARL LONG

~✦~

To err is Truman.—A popular joke in 1946

~✦~

Snarkin' the News

↔ A fifty-one-year-old Florida woman with cancer robbed a bank recently because "it was on my bucket list." . . . what, just above "die in prison"?

↔ Doesn't it sometimes feel like you're in the middle of a joke? Three women were arrested for showing up at a drug hearing carrying drugs. Included was a tourniquet, a syringe, a copious amount of pills, and some hash. Why not wear T-shirts that say "We have drugs"? Did they think the term "drug test" was going to be an oral exam? Or that the authorities would test their drugs for them, you know, for quality? Yikes.

↔ A group of Hasidic women chased down a twelve-year-old mugger, took his gun, and held him until the police came. When they finally arrived, the boy screamed, "Please, please take me to jail, I can't stand the guilt anymore!"

↔ Recently, a man was found bleeding from the head and, when asked what happened, told police he was pistol-whipped by his drug connection for trying to pay him with Monopoly money. Guess the dealer wanted Boardwalk and the two utilities as well.

↔ The town of Weed in California was the scene of the arrest of an outdoor writer who was running an enormous pot business out of his barn. I'm thinking a town called Weed would be the last place I would've set that up, no? The town has a population of 3,000 people and boasts 187 fast-food joints.

↔ Obscure reference #1: Jerry Brown is going to run for governor of California again and downloads of Linda Ronstadt's "You're No Good" have gone through the roof.

He's like the little man on top of the wedding cake.
—HAROLD ICKES

✦✦✦

He is just about the nastiest little man I've ever known.
He struts sitting down.
—LILLIAN DYKSTRA ABOUT THOMAS DEWEY

The youthful sparkle in his eyes is caused by his contact lenses, which he keeps highly polished.
—SHEILA GRAHAM ABOUT RONALD REAGAN

✦✦✦

He is brilliant—to the top of his boots.
—DAVID LLOYD GEORGE

✦✦

He is simply a shiver looking for a spine to run up.
—PAUL KEATING

~✦~

A guy walks past a mental hospital and hears a moaning voice "13 . . . 13 . . . 13 . . . 13" . . . The man looks over, sees a hole in the wall, looks through the hole and gets poked in the eye. "14 . . . 14 . . . 14 . . . 14."

~✦~

He knows nothing and thinks he knows everything. That points clearly to a political career.
—GEORGE BERNARD SHAW

✦✦✦

He's very clever, but sometimes his brains go to his head.
—MARGOT ASQUITH

right to my opinion. ✦ I wonder how many angels could dance on his head? ✦ I

Triumph the Insult Comic Dog [70]

↪ To an overweight person: "Are you a separatist? Maybe you should try separating yourself from doughnuts first."

↪ To a French person: "Pardon me, I only know your basic French expressions like 'I surrender.'"

↪ To a political consultant: "Here, I'll talk to your butt . . . I'm sorry, I forgot which side the poop comes out of."

You have all the characteristics of a popular politician: a horrible voice, bad breeding, and a vulgar manner.
—ARISTOPHANES

---

[70] Yeah, that's right. Sometimes dogs *are* smarter than you.

like to have the spitting concession on his grave. ◆ I'd rather pass a kidney ston

Sports

> Golf appeals to the idiot in us, and the child. Just how childlike golf players become is proven by their frequent inability to count past five.
> —JOHN UPDIKE

LIKE MANY AMERICANS, I love sports. Not all, mind you . . . just the good ones.

Inevitably, when I do get the time to settle back and watch an entire game (usually in a bar), my snark meter always goes off when I hear the idiotic interviews with key players or the insipid commentary from the broadcasters trying to fill the air. Banter has been made banal.

Sports and competition has always brought out that side of people that opens a clear path to snark, on the field and off. The quotes in this chapter shows that a sharp tongue can be a great weapon. Play ball!

Baseball without fans is like Jayne Mansfield without a
sweater. Hang on, that can be taken two ways.
—RICHARD NIXON

~♦~

Back in 1961 the Cincinnati Reds had a Vene-
zuelan shortstop named Elio Chacón, whose
command of the English language was limited,
and a Cuban coach named Reggie Otero with
much better bilingual skills. The story is that
one day an umpire made a questionable call
adverse to Chacón and the Reds and Chacón
went into a tirade in Spanish. The umpire
asked Otero, "Did he just call me what I think
he called me?" and Otero replied, "Oh no, he
doesn't know enough English to call you what
you are," and with that the umpire threw Otero
out of the game.

~♦~

Bruce Benedict is so slow he'd finish third in a race with a
pregnant woman.
—TOMMY LASORDA

♦♦♦

If you think it's hard to meet new people, try
picking up the wrong golf ball.
—JACK LEMMON

outta you, I'll squeeze your head.   ♦   If idiots could fly, this would be an airport.   ♦

Terry Bradshaw is so dumb, he couldn't spell
C–A–T if you spotted him the C and the A.
—THOMAS HENDERSON

~♦~

*Shelby Metcalf, basketball coach at Texas
A&M, recounting what he told a player who
received four Fs and one D: "Son, looks to
me like you're spending too much time on one
subject."*

~♦~

Dick Cheney's defense is that he was aiming at a quail when
he shot the guy. Which means that Cheney now has the
worst aim of anyone in the White House since Bill Clinton
—JAY LENO, COMMENTING ON THE VICE-PRESIDENT'S
HUNTING MISHAP, WHEN HE SHOT HIS FRIEND
INSTEAD OF A BIRD

~♦~

*What has four legs and no ears?
Mike Tyson's dog.*

~♦~

lose enough to him, you can hear the ocean. ♦ I'm glad to see you're not letting

Match the Insult to the Athlete[71]

A. Muhammed Ali   D. George Best

B. Torii Hunter   E. Maria Sharapova

C. Roy Keane   F. John McEnroe

~✦~

1. You were a crap player, you are a crap manager. The only reason I have any dealings with you is that somehow you are manager of my country and you're not even Irish, you English ****. You can stick it up your bollocks.
2. I'm not the next [Anna] Kournikova—I want to win matches.
3. Joe Frazier is so ugly he should donate his face to the U.S. Bureau of Wildlife.
4. What problems do you have, apart from being unemployed, a moron, and a dork?
5. He cannot kick with his left foot, he cannot head a ball, he cannot tackle, and he doesn't score many goals. Apart from that he's all right.
6. Why should I get this kid from the South Side of Chicago and have Scott Boras represent him and pay him $5 million when you can get a Dominican guy for a bag of chips?

---

[71] 1. C., 2. E., 3. A., 4. F., 5. D., 6. B.

your education get in the way of your ignorance. ✦ I'm going to memorize you

Putting allows the touchy golfer two to four opportunities
to blow a gasket in the short space of two to forty feet.
—TOMMY BOLT

++

What's the difference between a three-week-old puppy
and a sportswriter? In six weeks, the puppy stops whining.
—MIKE DITKA

+++

What's the penalty for killing a photographer?
One stroke or two?
—PRO GOLFER DAVIS LOVE III

++

Golf and sex are about the only things you can
enjoy without being good at.
—JIMMY DEMARET

+++

Golf is like chasing a quinine pill around a cow pasture.
—WINSTON CHURCHILL

++

I'm tired of hearing about money, money, money,
money, money. I just want to play the game, drink
Pepsi and wear Reebok.
—SHAQUILLE O'NEAL

~✦~

Sammy Davis was playing golf when the pro asked him his handicap. He replied, "I'm blind in one eye and a Jew."

~✦~

The people who gave us golf and called it a game are the same people who gave us bagpipes and called it music.

✦✦✦

As a boxer, he floats like a butterfly and stings like one, too.

✦✦

I would like to thank the press from the heart of my bottom.

—NICK FALDO AFTER WINNING THE 1992 OPEN

✦✦✦

I'm not saying my golf game went bad, but if I grew tomatoes, they'd come up sliced.

—LEE TREVINO

✦✦

Mr. Agnew, I believe you have a slight swing in your flaw.

—JIMMY DEMARET TO SPIRO T. AGNEW

half-wit is king. ✦ It is mind over matter. I don't mind, because you don't matter

~✦~

Boxing promoter Dan Duva on Mike Tyson going to prison: "Why would anyone expect him to come out smarter? He went to prison for three years, not Princeton."[72]

~✦~

Reporter to George Foreman after 1994 win against Michael Moorer: "Was the fight fixed?" Foreman's response: "Sure the fight was fixed. I fixed it with a right hand."

~✦~

Stu Grimson, Chicago Blackhawks left wing, explaining why he keeps a color photo of himself above his locker: "That's so when I forget how to spell my name, I can still find my clothes."

~✦~

Lou Duva, veteran boxing trainer, on the spartan training regime of heavyweight Andrew Golota: "He's a guy who gets up at six o'clock in the morning, regardless of what time it is."

~✦~

---

[72] Clearly a man with a death wish but the newer, gentler Mike would at least do it fast.

get the big picture when you have such a small screen. ✦ I've come across

~✦~

A man staggers into an emergency room with a concussion, multiple bruises, two black eyes, and a five iron wrapped tightly around his throat. Naturally, the doctor asks him what happened.

"Well, it was like this . . . I was having a quiet round of golf with my wife, when at a difficult hole we both sliced our balls into a pasture of cows. We went to look for them, and while I was rooting around, noticed one of the cows had something white at its rear end. I walked over and lifted up the tail, and sure enough, there was a golf ball with my wife's monogram on it, stuck right in the middle of the cow's butt, and that's when I made my mistake . . ."

"What did you do?," the doctor asked.

"I lifted the cow's tail again and yelled to my wife, 'Hey, this looks like yours!' . . . I don't remember much after that."

~✦~

Without the use of drugs our athletes are like drivers of a racing car with one gear less than their rivals.
—HARVEY SMITH

decomposed bodies that are less offensive than you are. ✦ I've only got one nerve l

Insults and More Insults

↔ If they can make penicillin out of moldy bread, they can sure make something out of you.[73]

↔ "My wife just had a baby." "Congratulations! Whose is it?"[74]

↔ Like an octopus falling out of a tree.[75]

↔ Lie down so I can recognize you.[76]

↔ He has so many hooks in his nose, he looks like a piece of bait.[77]

↔ She was so far in the closet she was in danger of being a garment bag.[78]

---

[73] Muhammad Ali to a young boxer
[74] Joe Frazier to Ken Norton
[75] David Feherty, the Irish former golfer, on Jim Furyk's swing
[76] Willie Pep, the American featherweight boxer, when asked by an old opponent if he remembered him
[77] Bob Costas about Dennis Rodman
[78] Rita Mae Brown about Martina Navratilova

Snarkin' the News

↔ Ain't sports grand? The general managers of all of the NHL hockey teams convened this week to decide which hits to the head would be deemed "illegal." Sort of conjures up one big Three Stooges convention, no? "Hey, Moe, pick two fingers. . . ."

↔ The leadoff batter for the Minnesota Twins hit a foul ball into the stands and struck his mother. He will spend the rest of the season in his room.

↔ Tiger Woods dropped out of the TPC because of a "bulge" in his neck. Wasn't a bulge what got him in trouble in the first place?

~•~

Torrin Polk, University of Houston receiver, on his coach, John Jenkins: "He treats us like men. He lets us wear earrings."

~•~

Football commentator and former player Joe Theismann: "Nobody in football should be called a genius. A genius is a guy like Norman Einstein."

~•~

becomes you—total darkness even more! • People say that you are the perfect idi

Sports

Senior basketball player at the University of Pittsburgh: "I'm going to graduate on time, no matter how long it takes."

~+~

If you're caught on a golf course during a storm and are afraid of lightning, hold up a 1-iron. Not even God can hit a 1-iron.
—LEE TREVINO

++

These greens are so fast I have to hold my putter over the ball and hit it with the shadow.
—SAM SNEAD

+++

I would like to deny all allegations by Bob Hope that during my last game of golf, I hit an eagle, a birdie, an elk, and a moose.
—GERALD FORD

++

Incompetence should not be confined to one sex.
—BILL RUSSELL ON FEMALES OFFICIATING IN THE NBA

+++

The Dodgers and Giants were playing in 1965, and Lou Johnson lined a ball into the seats down the left-field line. A blind man would've known it was foul, but third-base ump Augie Donatelli made the call anyway.

When the inning ended, Donatelli happened to look toward the stands where the ball went and saw stadium attendants carrying a woman on a stretcher.

As Junior Gilliam trotted out to play third for the Dodgers, Donatelli asked him, "Did Johnson's foul hit that woman?"

"Nah," Gilliam said. "You called it right, and she fainted."

~•~

Amarillo High School and Oiler coach Bum Phillips, when asked by Bob Costas why he takes his wife on all the road trips, responded: "Because she is too damn ugly to kiss good-bye."

~•~

And, upon hearing Joe Jacoby of the 'Skins say, "I'd run over my own mother to win the Super Bowl," Matt Millen of the Raiders said: "To win, I'd run over Joe's mom, too."

Things in Golf That Sound Dirty

1. After eighteen holes, I can barely walk.
2. You really whacked the hell out of that sucker.
3. Mind if I join your threesome?
4. Keep your head down and spread your legs a bit more.
5. Hold up . . . I need to wash my balls first.

You've got one problem—you stand too close
to the ball . . . after you've hit it.
—SAM SNEAD

~✦~

A look at the transcript from one Tiger Woods
interview:
Q: "Do you look forward to playing golf
again?"
A: "I dunno, for some reason eighteen holes
feels a little bit like a letdown."

~✦~

Fifty years ago, a hundred white men chasing one black
man across a field was called the Ku Klux Klan.
Today it's called the PGA Tour.
—UNKNOWN

~✦~

Shaquille O'Neal was having trouble with his free-throw shots. To rattle him, opposing player A. C. Greene, co-founder of the group Athletes for Abstinence, called out, "You'll be all right as soon as you get some experience." Shaq replied, "And you'll be okay as soon as you get some sex."

~✦~

The least thing upsets him on the links.
He missed short putts because of the uproar of butterflies
in the adjoining meadows.
—P. G. WODEHOUSE

was another one of his near Mrs. ✦ She's a lot like train tracks—she's been laid acro

CHARISMA

(OR LACK THEREOF)

ry. ◆ She's got a body that won't quit and a brain that won't start. ◆ She's like Taco

CHARISMA

OR LACK THEREOF

When you're annoying me, I'll let you know it. I think of it as community service, not as being mean. Because otherwise you'll just keep on doing it—your quirks, peculiarities, mannerisms, and traits, which may be cute to your mom[79] but aren't—and quickly everyone you know will be avoiding you like the swine flu. By nipping it in the bud, I'm preventing you from horrifying the entire world with your lack of style, taste, and personality, hence the "service" aspect of my advice. Don't try to convince yourself that it's me. Listen to what I'm saying and change.

You have an inferiority complex— and it's fully justified.

✦

You're not yourself today. I noticed the improvement immediately.

✦

I'm just trying to imagine you with a personality.

✦

Do you have to leave so soon? I was about to poison the tea.

✦

There are enough people to hate in the world already without you working so hard to give us another.

✦

Jesus loves you, but everyone else thinks you're an asshole.

---

[79] Maybe when you were a four-year-old . . .

Do you ever wonder what life would be like if you'd had enough oxygen at birth?

✦

Of course I'd like to help you out. Which way did you come in?

✦

You know the drill! You leave a message. . . . and I ignore it!

✦

If you see two people talking and one looks bored, he's the other one.

✦

I'm not mean . . . you're just a sissy.

When I think of all the people I respect the most, you're right there, serving them drinks.

I can't seem to remember your name, but please don't help me.

✦

I don't know what your problem is, but I'll bet it's hard to pronounce.

Of all the people I've met . . . you're certainly one of them.

are has-beens. You are a never-was. ✦ Talk is cheap, but so are you. ✦ The only t

Work

> The best way to appreciate your job is to
> imagine yourself without one.
> —OSCAR WILDE

W E ALL HATE WORK. We spend half of our lives there and are rarely satisfied. Anybody that says different is either lying, brain-dead, or an idiot. And ripe for a promotion.

We spend our days thinking of ways to get out of work. Feigning sickness, searching the Internet, leaving early. Everybody thinks their job is the worst, their workplace the most unhealthy, that their coworkers are the biggest schmucks . . . so I can't think of a better breeding ground for great snark . . . or a better place to use it.

It's a recession when your neighbor loses his job: it's a
depression when you lose yours.
—HARRY S. TRUMAN

✦✦✦

Snarky Workplace Commentary

↝ Errors have been made. Others will be blamed.

↝ Can I trade this job for what's behind Door One?

↝ Too many freaks, not enough circuses.

↝ Chaos, panic, and disorder—my work here is done.

↝ I thought I wanted a career, turns out I just wanted
the paychecks.

↝ Sarcasm is just one more service we offer.

↝ How many people work in your office? About half
of them.

↝ Out of my mind. Back in five minutes.

↝ There's too much blood in my caffeine system.

↝ You set low standards and consistently fail to
achieve them.

If A equals success, then the formula is A equals X plus Y and Z, with X being work, Y play, and Z keeping your mouth shut.

—ALBERT EINSTEIN

✦✦

I have plenty of talent and vision. I just don't give a damn.

✦✦✦

How do I set a laser printer to stun?

✦✦

Doing nothing is very hard to do . . . you never know when you're finished.

—LESLIE NIELSEN

✦✦✦

Today is "Take our Daughters to Work Day." This is when girls ages nine to fifteen go to work. Or, as it's called at the Nike factory—Thursday.

—BILL MAHER

✦✦

A good rule of thumb is if you've made it to thirty-five and your job still requires you to wear a name tag, you've made a serious vocational error.

—DENNIS MILLER

that I find obnoxious, and you are all of them. ✦ There is no vaccine against

Match the Insult to the Businessman[80]

A. Donald Trump   D. Bill Gates

B. Steve Jobs   E. Ted Turner

C. Henry Ford   F. Warren Buffett

~•~

1. Be nice to nerds. Chances are you'll end up working for one.
2. Let blockheads read what blockheads wrote.
3. My son is now an "entrepreneur." That's what you're called when you don't have a job.
4. I have made the tough decisions, always with an eye toward the bottom line. Perhaps it's time America was run like a business.
5. Pretty much, Apple and Dell are the only ones in this industry making money. They make it by being Walmart. We make it by innovation.
6. A business that makes nothing but money is a poor business.

The only place where success comes before work is in the dictionary.
—DONALD KENDALL

---

[80] 1. D., 2. F., 3. E., 4. A., 5. B., 6. C.

stupidity. ◆ Thinking isn't your strong suit, is it? ◆ This is no battle of wits betwe

~✦~

A manager is called into his boss's office on Monday and told he has to get rid of one employee in his department. "Downsizing." He's really upset. For the next two days he racks his brain trying to figure out whom to fire. On Tuesday afternoon he sees Jack and Jill standing at the watercooler. He says to himself, "Okay, it's going to be one of them." He spends the next few days scrutinizing what each of them does. Everything is equal. Productivity. Time off. Reports. Everything. He's in a quandary. It's Friday afternoon and he knows he's going to have to think about this all weekend. Everyone has left the office except Jack and Jill, who are getting ready to leave. She comes over to say good-bye.

"Have a good weekend, boss. Hey, you don't look so good. Is everything okay?"

He looks at her and says, "To be honest, I'm having a tough time here. I can't decide if I should lay you or Jack off."

She looks at him and says, "Well, I have to catch a bus, so I suggest you jack off."

~✦~

e. I never pick on an unarmed man. ✦ We know that you would go to the end of the

The reward for work well done is
the opportunity to do more.

+++

Experience is a comb that nature gives
to men when they are bald.

++

Things Not to Say to Your Boss

- ↝ I wasn't sleeping . . . I was testing my keyboard for drool resistance.

- ↝ Yes, I can only do one thing at a time. . . . I could do more with a raise, though.

- ↝ There is nothing left on YouTube to watch!

- ↝ Hey, I just took this job for the high-speed Internet.

- ↝ I wasn't daydreaming. Do you discriminate against people who practice yoga?

- ↝ That's what I like about working for you: total freedom from hero worship. It's refreshing.

- ↝ I'm not doodling, I thought you were gone for the day.

- ↝ I have the power to channel my imagination into ever-soaring levels of suspicion and paranoia.

world for us. But would you stay there? • What he lacks in intelligence, he mor

Ambition is a poor excuse for not having sense
enough to be lazy.
—CHARLIE McCARTHY

✦✦✦

An expert is someone called in at the
last minute to share the blame.

✦✦

Snarky Definitions

Concept, *n.*: Any *idea* for which an outside consultant billed you more than $25,000.

Entrepreneur, *n.*: A high-rolling risk taker who would rather be a spectacular failure than a dismal success.

Expert, *n.*: Someone who comes from out of town and shows slides.

Memo, *n.*: An interoffice communication too often written more for the benefit of the person who sends it than the person who receives it.

~✦~

Q. What do your boss and a Slinky have in common?
A. They're both fun to watch tumble down the stairs.

~✦~

His insomnia was so bad, he couldn't sleep
during office hours.
—ARTHUR BAER

✦✦

Any organization is like a septic tank. The really big chunks
rise to the top.
—JOHN IMHOFF

✦✦✦

Snarkin' the News

↦ Key jobs predicted for the future: Lawyers specializing in gay divorce and tattoo removal artists. Other futuristic opportunities—Facebook twelve-step program leaders, doctors specializing in Wii-related injuries, and used e-booksellers.

↦ Honda has announced it is expanding its recall of airbag inflators and will now need to get back the ones they lent to Congress immediately.

you like some cheese and crackers to go with that whine? ✦ You are no longer benea

↝ Bernie Madoff's family petitioned the court this week to change their name to Morgan, claiming they were being harassed when people heard the name. They choose Morgan as an homage to J. P. Morgan, a robber baron who bilked millions out of their hard-earned money.

↝ *The Wall Street Journal* reports that the price of cars is going up. Toyota is now charging extra for brakes.

↝ Scientists have discovered that the thawing permafrost is releasing nitrous oxide into the ozone. This explains the uncontrollable laughter coming from people in Greenland as they freeze their asses off.

It's not so much how busy you are, but why you are busy.
The bee is praised, the mosquito is swatted.
—CATHERINE O'HARA

✦✦

The status of a temp is somewhere between that of a security guard and the crud behind the refrigerator.
—SCOTT ADAMS

✦✦✦

Nothing is illegal if a hundred businessmen decide to do it, and that's true anywhere in the world.
—ANDREW YOUNG

~◆~

Two guys are running a store and decide to have a big clearance sale. Within three hours, everything is sold from the store. One fellow says to the other, "Well, what now? We've sold everything."

The other replies, "Don't worry, there's a guy who comes in here every day and ask stupid questions. We'll have a few laughs on him."

Sure enough, the guy comes walking in, hands in pockets, looking around. "Tell me, what's on sale today?"

One of the fellows says, "Hey, just in time, we're having a sale on assholes!"

To which the guy replies, "Well, ya must be doing pretty good, 'cause ya only got two left!"

~◆~

A cubicle is just a padded cell without a door.

◆◆

I have a degree in liberal arts. Do you
want fries with that?

◆◆◆

I work hard because millions on welfare depend upon me.

◆◆

I'm just working here until a good fast-food job
opens up.

her in the river and skim ugly for two days. ◆ You have a speech impediment . .

~✦~

An air freshener salesman goes to an executive building to market his product to a prospective buyer. He steps in to an empty elevator and presses the tenth-floor button. Just as the doors close, he lets out an awful fart.

The elevator stops on the fifth floor, so he quickly sprays his new "Pine-scented" air freshener to cover his tracks. The doors open and a man steps onto the elevator.

The salesman figures this is a good opportunity to test his product's quality, so he says, "Excuse me, sir, could you kindly tell me what you smell?"

The man replies, "Yeah, smells like someone shit a Christmas tree."

~✦~

One man alone can be pretty dumb
sometimes, but for real bona fide stupidity there
ain't nothing can beat teamwork.
—*THE MONKEY WRENCH GANG*

✦✦

A committee is a cul-de-sac down which ideas are
lured and then quietly strangled.
—SIR BARNETT COCKS

✦ You have a striking face. Tell me, how many times were you struck there? ✦ You

Most of what we call management consists of making it
difficult for people to get their work done.
—PETER F. DRUCKER

~•~

*An elephant and a camel are waiting to be
interviewed for the same job. The elephant
asked: "Why are your tits on your back?" "I
don't know," said the camel. "Why is your dick
on your face?"*

~•~

Employee of the month is a good example of how somebody
can be both a winner and a loser at the same time.
—DEMETRI MARTIN

••

A secretary ran into the boss's office and said
"Can I use your Dictaphone?"
He said, "No, use your finger like everybody else."
—BERNARD MANNING

••

Ambition is the last refuge of the failure.
—OSCAR WILDE

possess a mind not merely twisted, but actually sprained. • You remind me of the oc

More Snarky Workplace Commentary,

- ↪ Ah . . . I see the fuck-up fairy has visited us again . . .

- ↪ I see you've set aside this special time to humiliate yourself in public.

- ↪ It sounds like English, but I can't understand a word you're saying.

- ↪ I can see your point, but I still think you're full of shit.

- ↪ You are validating my inherent mistrust of strangers.

- ↪ Thank you. We're all refreshed and challenged by your unique point of view.

- ↪ Yes, I am an agent of Satan, but my duties are largely ceremonial.

- ↪ No, my powers can only be used for good.

- ↪ Who, me? I just wander from room to room.

ake me sick. ✦ You say that you are always bright and early. Well, okay, we know

Snarkin' the News

↔ The Wilhelmina Modeling agency is having financial difficulties and is in the process of making major cuts to stay in business. Most dramatic: The food budget for a photo shoot has been slashed from $8 to $3.

↔ A waitress in PA will be brought up on fraud charges after she was spotted dancing at a gentleman's club after collecting $27K in disability checks for a back injury . . . hey, be fair. . . . You know how hard it is to work the pole in a back brace?

↔ A sailor weighing anchor in Austria brought up a sunken BMW—with the dead driver still behind the wheel—and still on his cell phone.

↔ Joe the Plumber said John McCain "screwed up his life." He has been consistently late for appointments, forgets to put the exact materials on his truck, overcharges people . . . and other unusual behaviors for plumbers. No other comments were forthcoming, as reporters tried to call him on the weekend.

↪ Idiots of the Month Club: Two men in Pennsylvania carjacked a pizza delivery truck but had to escape on foot when they both realized neither knew how to drive a stick shift.

↪ A man walked into a restaurant that was closing and asked for some napkins. The owner refused and told him to leave. The man picked up a saltshaker and threw it at the owner, hitting him in the face and breaking his nose. He was arrested and charged with aggravated a-salt.

Employees make the best dates. You don't have to pick them up, and they're always tax-deductible.
—ANDY WARHOL

~◆~

Reporter: "What do you look for in a script?"
Spencer Tracy: "Days off."

~◆~

you look terrible in the light. • You started at the bottom—and it's been downhi

Love and Hate

Sometimes I need what only you can provide:
your absence.
—ASHLEIGH BRILLIANT

THERE IS A VERY fine line between friends and enemies and between marriage and divorce. The balance is precarious at best. Bitter friends, bosom enemies. Loving husband, dearest wife . . . two dogs at each other's throats.

The snarks in this chapter are subtle but loaded. Keep in mind that this is an area where the consequences can be dire, so choose the level of snark wisely. After all, love is grand, but divorce is a hundred grand.

• You used to be arrogant and obnoxious. Now you are just the opposite. You are

The history of women is the history of the worst
tyranny the world has ever known: the tyranny of
the weak over the strong. It is the only tyranny
that ever lasts.

—OSCAR WILDE[81]

✦✦

I consider that women who are authors,
lawyers, and politicians are monsters.

—AUGUSTE RENOIR

✦✦✦

I never married because there was no need. I have three
pets at home, which answer the same purpose as a
husband. I have a dog which growls every morning, a
parrot which swears all afternoon, and a cat that comes
home late at night.

—MARIE CORELLI

✦✦

Women want mediocre men, and men are working hard to
become as mediocre as possible.

—MARGARET MEAD

✦✦✦

We've been through so much together, and most
of it was your fault.

—ASHLEIGH BRILLIANT

---

[81] Leave it to a gay man to appreciate the plight of women.

obnoxious and arrogant. ✦ You're a habit I'd like to kick, with both feet. ✦ You're l

Signs Your Family Is Stressed

1. Conversations begin with "Put down the gun and we can talk."
2. People have trouble understanding your kids because they talk through clenched teeth.
3. No one has time to wait for microwave TV dinners.
4. Family meetings are mediated by law enforcement.
5. You are trying to get your four-year-old to switch to decaf.

The last guy I went out with, he was just so—I don't know—
hopeless. He said if I broke up with him that he would kill
himself. And I broke up with him, but he's not dead yet. I
want to call him up and be like, "You know, what's the deal?
I thought we had an agreement."

—MARGARET CHO

+++

We seem to be going through all the traditional stages of a
marriage. She recently went through the "faking a headache"
stage. Now she's going through the "I find you physically
repugnant" stage. I miss the headache stage.

—JONATHAN KATZ

se "idiots savants," except without the "savant" part. • You're so dumb you thought

~•~

A stranger was seated next to John on the plane. The stranger turned to John and said, "Let's talk. I've heard that flights will go quicker if you strike up a conversation with your fellow passenger."

John, who had just opened his book, closed it slowly, and said to the stranger, "What would you like to discuss?"

"Oh, I don't know," said the stranger. "How about nuclear power?"

"Okay," said John. "That could be an interesting topic. But let me ask you a question first. A horse, a cow, and a deer all eat grass. The same stuff. Yet a deer excretes little pellets, while a cow turns out a flat patty, and a horse produces clumps of dried grass. Why do you suppose that is?"

"Jeez," said the stranger. "I have no idea."

"Well, then," said John, "How is it that you feel qualified to discuss nuclear power when you don't know shit?"

~•~

With a big guy, it's good. You always know when he's ready
for sex, 'cause naked, he looked like one of them Butterball
turkeys with the little pop-up timer.
—LISA LAMPANELLI

◆◆◆

If you can't live without me, why aren't
you dead already?
—CYNTHIA HEIMEL

◆◆

Some of my best leading men have been
dogs and horses.
—ELIZABETH TAYLOR

◆◆◆

A woman's mind is cleaner than a man's.
She changes it more often.
—OLIVER HERFORD

◆◆

He was happily married—but his wife wasn't.
—VICTOR BORGE

◆◆◆

A wife of forty should be like money. You should be able to
change her for two twenties.

Match the Insult to the Person[82]

A. Edward G. Bulwer-Lytton   D. Rod Stewart

B. Katharine Hepburn   E. Leonard Louis

C. Roseanne Barr   Levinson

                           F. Zsa Zsa Gabor

~+~

1. My husband and I didn't sign a prenuptial agreement. We signed a mutual suicide pact.
2. Getting divorced just because you don't love a man is almost as silly as getting married just because you do.
3. It is difficult to say who do you the most harm: enemies with the worst intentions or friends with the best.
4. If you want to sacrifice the admiration of many men for the criticism of one, go ahead, get married.
5. Instead of getting married, I'm going to find a woman I don't like and just give her a house.
6. He is a fine friend. He stabs you in the front.

Pushing forty? She's hanging on for dear life.
—IVY COMPTON-BURNETT

---

[82]   1. C., 2. F., 3. A., 4. B., 5. D., 6. E.

~♦~

A young boy's mother was cleaning Junior's room one day and found a bondage S&M magazine, some rope, leather gear, and similar items. When she showed it to her husband, he handed it back to her without a word. She finally asked, "What should we do about this?" He looked at her and said, "Well, I don't think you should spank him."

—FRIARS CLUB JOKE

~♦~

She's been married so many times she has rice
marks on her face.
—HENNY YOUNGMAN

♦♦♦

She's got such a narrow mind, when she
walks fast her earrings bang together.
—JOHN CANTU

♦♦

She not only kept her lovely figure, she's added so much to it.
—BOB FOSSE

♦♦♦

Outside every thin girl is a fat man, trying to get in.
—KATHARINE WHITEHORN

over the cord of a cellular phone. ♦ You've got your head so far up your ass you can

Snarky Toasts

↔ To marriage . . . the rest period between romance.

↔ To marriage . . . to some a small word, to others a long sentence.

↔ A wedding ring is like a tourniquet; it cuts off circulation.

↔ Without marriage, men and women would have to fight with total strangers.

↔ May all your ups and downs be between the sheets.

↔ Always talk to your wife during lovemaking . . . if there's a phone handy.

↔ To our wives and lovers . . . may they never meet.

↔ May bad fortune follow you all the days of your life . . . and never catch up to you.

↔ To birthdays . . . not so bad considering the alternative.

↔ To friends . . . and the strength to put up with them.

chew your food twice. • You've never been outspoken; no one has ever been

Marriage is neither heaven nor hell, it is simply purgatory.
—ABRAHAM LINCOLN

··

I think the best part of being gay is when you're done, you
could turn over and talk about football.
—ANDREW DICE CLAY

~·~

*A husband gets home from work and finds his
wife in bed with his best friend. Anger gets the
best of him, and he grabs his gun from the closet
and shoots the man dead. His wife shakes her
head in despair and says, "If you keep behaving
like this, you'll lose all your friends!"*

~·~

Marriage is a three-ring circus: engagement ring,
wedding ring, and suffering.

···

Love your enemies . . . it pisses them off.

··

She can break her standards faster than she can lower them.

···

Women priests. Great.
Now there's priests of both sexes I don't listen to.
—BILL HICKS

You're the best at all you do—and all you do is make people hate you.   ·   I have a

~✦~

A woman is standing in a crowded elevator of the hotel she's staying in when a man walks in and accidentally elbows her. He says "I'm sorry! But if your heart is as soft as your breast, you'll forgive me." The woman replies, "If your dick is as hard as your elbow, I'm in room 27."

~✦~

He made enemies as naturally as soap makes suds.
—PERCIVAL WILDE

✦✦

An open marriage is nature's way of telling
you that you need a divorce.
—ANN LANDERS

~✦~

A husband and wife are in bed watching Who Wants to be a Millionaire? *The husband asks for sex. The wife says, "No." Her husband asks, "Is that your final answer?" She responds, "Yes." He says, "Then, I'd like to phone a friend."*

~✦~

I've had many cases of love that were just infatuation, but
this hate I feel for you is the real thing.

✦✦✦

It's men like you that give the Y chromosome a bad name.

computer, a vibrator, and pizza delivery. Why should I leave the house? ✦ Stress is

You are so two-faced that any woman who married you would be married to a bigamist.

✦✦

What's the maximum punishment for bigamy? Two mothers-in-law.

~✦~

A blonde calls her boyfriend and says, "Please come over here and help me. I have a killer jigsaw puzzle, and I can't figure out how to get it started." Her boyfriend asks, "What is it supposed to be when it's finished?" The blonde says, "According to the picture on the box, it's a tiger." Her boyfriend decides to go over and help with the puzzle. She lets him in and shows him where she has the puzzle spread all over the table. He studies the pieces for a moment, then turns to her and says, "First of all, no matter what we do, we're not going to be able to assemble these pieces into anything resembling a tiger." He holds her hand softly, leads her to a chair, and says, "Second, I'd advise you to relax. Let's have a cup of coffee, and then. . . ." He sighs, "Let's put all these Frosted Flakes back in the box."

~✦~

A lawyer is never entirely comfortable with
a friendly divorce, any more than a good mortician
wants to finish his job and then have the patient sit
up on the table.
—JEAN KERR

++

The difference between divorce and legal separation is that a
legal separation gives a husband time to hide his money.
—JOHNNY CARSON

+++

Just another of our many disagreements. He wants a
no-fault divorce, whereas I would prefer to have
the bastard crucified.
—J. B. HANDELSMAN

++

A man is in general better pleased when he has a good
dinner upon his table, than when his wife talks Greek.
—SAMUEL JOHNSON

+++

A woman is only a woman, but a good cigar is a smoke.
—RUDYARD KIPLING, LATER USED BY GROUCHO MARX

++

In order to avoid being called a flirt,
she always yielded easily.
—CHARLES, COUNT TALLEYRAND

~+~

During a heated spat over finances a husband said, "Well, if you'd learn to cook and were willing to clean this place, we could fire the maid." His wife, fuming, shot back, "Oh yeah?!? Well, if you'd learn how to fuck, we could fire the chauffeur and the gardener."

~+~

Brigands demand your money or your life.
Women demand both.
—SAMUEL BUTLER

~+~

Female teetotaler: "I would rather commit adultery than take a glass of beer."
Man, overhearing her: "Who wouldn't?"

~+~

God created Adam, lord of all living creatures,
but Eve spoiled it all.
—MARTIN LUTHER

ar the pitter-patter of little feet, I'll put shoes on my cats. ✦ Do I look like a people

~•~

Q: Why are most serial killers men?
A: Because woman like to kill one man slowly,
over many years.

~•~

Give a man a free hand and he'll run it all over you.
—MAE WEST

•••

Bride; n. A woman with a fine prospect of
happiness behind her.
—AMBROSE BIERCE

••

I sometimes think that God, in creating man, somewhat
overestimated his ability.
—OSCAR WILDE

•••

Your idea of fidelity is not having more than one man in bed
at the same time.
—FREDERIC RAPHAEL

••

[My boyfriend's] not technically a lawyer, but he's got three
court cases next week.
—LISA LAMPANELLI

•••

He's been trying to drown his sorrows for years—but she's
too good a swimmer.

person? • This isn't an office. It's hell with fluorescent lighting. • A hard-on doesn't (

Things Men Would Do with a Vagina for a Day

1. Immediately go shopping for cucumbers and zucchini.
2. Squat over a handheld mirror for an hour.
3. See if it's possible to launch a Ping-Pong ball twenty feet.
4. Finally find that damned G-spot.

Things Women Would Do with a Penis for a Day

1. Get ahead faster in corporate America.
2. Get a blow job.
3. Pee standing.
4. Jump up and down naked with an erection to see if it feels as funny as it looks.
5. Repeat number 2.

He may have married her for her looks, but not the one she's giving him now.

She could marry any man she pleased. Unfortunately, she hasn't pleased one yet.

~+~

A couple drove down a country road for several miles, not saying a word. An earlier discussion had led to an argument, and neither of them wanted to concede their position. As they passed a barnyard of mules, goats, and pigs, the husband asked sarcastically, "Relatives of yours?" "Yep," the wife replied, "in-laws."

~+~

Between men and women there is no friendship possible. There is passion, enmity, worship, love, but no friendship.

—OSCAR WILDE

++

perfume. Must you marinate in it? • The difference between this company and a c

BODY
(OR LACK THEREOF)

BODY

OR LACK THEREOF

Think you're too fat? Too skinny? Too tall or too short? Too sweaty? Too wrinkled? Imagine what Spanx would do if we got all Zen on our looks. Don't worry, I'm not going soft on you. It's not going to happen unless we suddenly enjoy looking like we're at Friendly's on a Sunday afternoon. (Ever driven by one of those joints? It's not pretty.) Sometimes you just want to vent. Or rant. Or lay it on the line. Sometimes you want to scream, "Hey, how about a salad?" or "Have you heard about this new thing called soap?" or "Say, can I buy you some gum or a package of breath mints?" or just plain "Get away from me. You smell." There's got to be a better way . . .

She lost 100 pounds, but that's because she was poached for ivory.

+

Hey, you have something on your chin . . . the third one down.

+

Can fat people go skinny-dipping?

+

Look at the bright side . . . fat people are harder to kidnap.

+

They said you were a great asset. I told them they were off by two letters.

+

If you didn't have feet, you wouldn't wear shoes . . . so why wear a bra?

Dancing with her was like moving a piano.

✦

How would you like to feel the way you look?

✦

I may be fat, but you're ugly, and I can lose weight.

✦

No, those pants don't make you look fatter. I mean, how could they?

✦

You're so fat, your car has stretch marks.

His dog fantasizes about other legs when he humps his.

✦

Beer with no alcohol is like a nun with a D-cup.

✦

It ain't the size, it's . . . no, it's the size.

___

If you're worried about criticism, sometimes a diet is the best defense.[83]

___

[83] *Arrested Development*

Mix is not a CD for cats. • That's it, no more free will. • You're special . . . and I mea

Life and Death

Either he's dead, or my watch has stopped.
—GROUCHO MARX

WHEN IT COMES TO these two things, life and death, no one's got a clue. Oh, everyone has an opinion and usually feels little compunction about sharing that opinion with you, regardless of how loudly thou doth protest. . . .

What to do about all that whining[84] . . . I say snark and snark hard. Stop 'em in their tracks. Put the kibosh on it. Pull the rug out from under 'em. . . . slay 'em. (Not literally, mind you.) Irony on a base level but still good stuff.

---

[84] Because by now you've set yourself up as Mr.-Your-Opinion-Doesn't-Matter.

He is useless on top of the ground; he ought to be under it,
inspiring the cabbages.
—MARK TWAIN

✦✦✦

If you can't be a good example, then you'll just have to be a
horrible warning.
—CATHERINE AIRD

✦✦

He would make a lovely corpse.
—CHARLES DICKENS

✦✦✦

He is an old bore. Even the grave yawns for him.
—HERBERT BEERBOHM TREE

~✦~

*A lifelong Republican was lying on his deathbed
when he suddenly decided to join the Democrats. "But why?" asked his puzzled friend,
"You're Republican through and through . . .
Why change now?" The man leaned forward
and explained, "Well, I'd rather it was one of
them that died and not one of us."*

~✦~

The years between fifty and seventy are the hardest.
You are always being asked to do things, and yet
you are not decrepit enough to turn them down.
—T. S. ELIOT

✦✦✦

My mother always said that every time you do a good
deed here on Earth, you're storing up a treasure in
heaven. Which means Mother Teresa's probably got some
beachfront property up there and I'm up to a box of Milk
Duds and a Pez dispenser.
—ROBERT G. LEE

✦✦

A lot of people say they think that Los Angeles is a heartless
place that breeds insincerity and mistrust. But you know, I
found that when I first moved there, I didn't like it, but after
a while, something inside me died.
—JAKE JOHANNSEN

✦✦✦

End of season sale at the cerebral department.
—GARETH BLACKSTOCK

✦✦

His mind is open . . . so open that ideas simply
pass through it.
—F. H. BRADLEY

oduce my selves. ✦ And which dwarf are you? ✦ Are those your eyeballs? I found

Woody Allen

↻ Life is divided into the horrible and the miserable.

↻ Life is full of misery, loneliness, and suffering—and it's all over much too soon.

↻ My one regret in life is that I am not someone else.

↻ On the plus side, death is one of the few things that can be done just as easily lying down.

↻ Why are our days numbered and not, say, lettered?

↻ I don't believe in an afterlife, although I am bringing a change of underwear.

↻ You can live to be a hundred if you give up all the things that make you want to live to be a hundred.

She's a waterbug on the surface of life.
—GLORIA STEINEM

✦✦✦

Stay with me; I want to be alone.
—JOEY ADAMS

them in my cleavage. ✦ Did I mention the kick in the groin you'll be receiving if you t

Match the Person to His Final Words[85]

A. Louis B. Mayer   D. Humphrey Bogart

B. Lady Nancy Astor   E. James W. Rodgers

C. Carl Panzram   F. Winston Churchill

~✦~

1. I should never have switched from Scotch to martinis.
2. I'm bored with it all.
3. Hurry it up you Hoosier bastard! I could hang a dozen men while you're screwing around.
4. Am I dying, or is this my birthday?
5. It wasn't worth it.
6. A bulletproof vest. (Asked if he has any last requests before facing a firing squad.)

Good news for senior citizens: Death is near!
—GEORGE CARLIN

✦✦

I never wanted to see anybody die, but there are a few
obituary notices I have read with pleasure.
—CLARENCE DARROW

---

[85] 1. D. , 2. F., 3. C., 4. B., 5. A., 6. E.

✦ Did the aliens forget to remove your anal probe? ✦ Does your train of thought

~•~

A woman went into a hospital to have her wrinkles removed but woke up to find the surgeon gave her breast implants. "What have you done?" she screamed. "I came in here to have the lines taken out, but instead you've given me these huge breasts!" "Hey," said the surgeon, "at least nobody's looking at your wrinkles anymore."

~•~

They say such nice things about people at their
funerals that it makes me sad that I'm going to
miss mine by just a few days.
—GARRISON KEILLOR

•••

Every creature stalks some other, and
catches it, and is caught.
—MIGNON McLAUGHLIN

••

She never was really charming till she died.
—TERENCE

•••

He would stab his best friend for the sake of writing
an epigram on his tombstone.
—OSCAR WILDE

Things Not to Say at a Funeral

↪ I should have said something earlier . . . but I really, really need his kidney.

↪ Whoa. I didn't know we were supposed to dress up.

↪ You look like you've seen a ghost.

↪ Boy, you wouldn't believe the day I'm having.

↪ Pull my finger.

↪ See, kids? This is what God does to the bad ones.

↪ Who needs gum?

Could I drop you off somewhere—say, the roof?

◆◆

Not all men are annoying. Some are dead.

◆◆◆

Death is hereditary.

◆◆

How do you save a man from drowning?
Take your foot off his head.

me. ◆ I started out with nothing and still have most of it left. ◆ If I throw a stick,

He is as good as his word—and his word is no good.
—SEAMUS McMANUS

+++

I wish I'd known you when you were alive.
—LEONARD LOUIS LEVINSON

~+~

Larry King: "You don't look ninety."
Milton Berle: "I don't feel it."
King: "How old do you feel?"
Berle: "I feel like a twenty-year-old—but there's
never one around."

~+~

I don't mind dying, the trouble is you feel so bloody stiff the
next day.
—GEORGE AXELROD

++

If no one knows when a person is going to
die, how can we say he died prematurely?
—GEORGE CARLIN

+++

A dead atheist is someone who is all dressed up
with no place to go.
—JAMES DUFFECY

will you leave?   ◆   I'm not your type. I'm not inflatable.   ◆   Macho Law prohibits me f

~✦~

When her husband passed away, the wife put the usual death notice in the newspaper, but added that he had died of gonorrhea. Once the daily newspapers had been delivered, a good friend of the family phoned and complained bitterly, "You know very well that he died of diarrhea, not gonorrhea."

Replied the widow, "Yes, I know that he died of diarrhea, but I thought it would be better for posterity to remember him as a great lover rather than the big shit that he really was."

~✦~

Afraid of death? Not at all. Be a great relief.
Then I wouldn't have to talk to you.
—KATHARINE HEPBURN

✦✦

My uncle Sammy was an angry man. He had printed on his
tombstone: What are you looking at?
—MARGARET SMITH

✦✦✦

At my age I do what Mark Twain did. I get my daily
paper, look at the obituaries page, and if I'm not
there, I carry on as usual.
—PATRICK MOORE

itting I'm wrong. ✦ Meandering to a different drummer. ✦ See no evil, hear no evil,

You should never say bad things about the dead, you should
only say good . . . Joan Crawford is dead. Good.
—BETTE DAVIS ABOUT JOAN CRAWFORD

••

I hate funerals and would not attend my own
if it could be avoided.
—ROBERT T. MORRIS

•••

The world is rid of him, but the deadly slime of
his touch remains.
—JOHN CONSTABLE ON LORD BYRON

••

I have lost friends, some by death—others by sheer inability
to cross the street.
—VIRGINIA WOOLF

•••

I am ready to meet my maker, but whether my
maker is prepared for the great ordeal of meeting
me is another matter.
—WINSTON CHURCHILL

••

He must have killed a lot of men
to have made so much money.
—MOLIÈRE

Epitaphs

Here lies my wife: here let her lie. Now she's at rest
and so am I.
—JOHN DRYDEN

✦✦✦

Where his soul's gone or how it fares; nobody
knows, and nobody cares.
—ANONYMOUS

✦✦

Hotten Rotten Forgotten.
—ON JOHN HOTTEN

✦✦✦

✦ The Bible was written by the same people who said the Earth was flat. ✦ You . . .

Off my planet! · No, you idiot, Meow Mix is not a CD for cats. · When you g

In Conclusion

S O I SAY UNTO thee, snark! And it will set you free!

(Always wanted to do that . . . you know . . . in a big voice like those preachers that dress like pimps? Falwell and those guys. . .)

Is there anything we've learned here? Yeah, there's a lot of people with huge bugs up their asses, no? Including yours truly. . . .

The difference is in finding a way to channel that angst and anger *at the time* and come back quickly with just the perfect amount of snark in your voice and words. It will set you free. Or send you to prison.

Say hey to Bubba for me.

en's room, you will see a sign that says, "Gentlemen." Pay no heed to it. Go right on

in. ♦ A well-balanced person with a chip on both shoulders. ♦ Another dopeless

Acknowledgments

I AM GRATEFUL FOR THE friendship and support of three brilliant people who have been through this before: My wife Rosalind, who has the patience of a saint and a snarky sense of humor all her own; my editor, Ann Treistman, who kept me on track, gave me lots of encouragement and kicked my ass when necessary; and Mark Mirando, a great friend with a wit to match.

Throughout the writing of this book, a number of folks looked at what I was doing and helped me shape the content. They are: my mom Janet, James Naccarato, John and Jenny Morris, Mike Jones, David Gilson, Bill Rafaelle, Glen Greenberg and the amazingly snarky staff at the Owl Bar, the incomparable Omuni Barnes and everyone at GPP, Tony Lyons and the Skyhorse gang, Karen Patterson and Stephanie Beam, and a host of many others who were there when needed.

1! ✦ Are you always an idiot, or just when I'm around? ✦ If you want to get laid, crawl

up a chicken's ass and wait! • Tell me the story of that dress. It's obviously an old favc

Index

were wise to remove the curtain rings. ✦ May your soul rest in eternal piss. ✦ You

you to turn the other cheek; it's just as ugly.   •   I don't know what makes you so stupid, |

ense of humor. ✦ You can't fix stupid. ✦ You must be from the shallow end of the gene pool. ◆ I'd explain it to you, but your brain would explode. ◆ You sound reasonable

♦ He has an intellect rivaled only by garden tools.